NEW DIRECTIONS FOR INSTITUTIONAL RESEARCH

Patrick T. Terenzini, *The Pennsylvania State University*
EDITOR-IN-CHIEF

Providing Useful Information for Deans and Department Chairs

Mary K. Kinnick
Portland State University

EDITOR

NUMBER 84, WINTER 1994

JOSSEY-BASS PUBLISHERS
San Francisco

PROVIDING USEFUL INFORMATION FOR
DEANS AND DEPARTMENT CHAIRS
Mary K. Kinnick (ed.)
New Directions for Institutional Research, no. 84
Volume XVI, Number 4
Patrick T. Terenzini, Editor-in-Chief

Microfilm copies of issues and articles are available in 16mm and 35mm,
as well as microfiche in 105mm, through University Microfilms Inc., 300
North Zeeb Road, Ann Arbor, Michigan 48106-1346.

LC 85-645339   ISSN 0271-0579   ISBN 0-7879-9989-X

NEW DIRECTIONS FOR INSTITUTIONAL RESEARCH is part of The Jossey-Bass
Higher and Adult Education Series and is published quarterly by Jossey-
Bass Inc., Publishers, 350 Sansome Street, San Francisco, California
94104-1342 (publication number USPS 098-830). Second-class postage
paid at San Francisco, California, and at additional mailing offices. POST-
MASTER: Send address changes to New Directions for Institutional
Research, Jossey-Bass Inc., Publishers, 350 Sansome Street, San Francisco,
California 94104-1342.

SUBSCRIPTIONS for 1994 cost $47.00 for individuals and $62.00 for institutions, agencies, and libraries.

EDITORIAL CORRESPONDENCE should be sent to the editor-in-chief, Patrick
T. Terenzini, Center for the Study of Higher Education, The Pennsylvania
State University, 403 South Allen Street, Suite 104, University Park,
Pennsylvania 16801-5202.

Photograph of the library by Michael Graves at San Juan Capistrano by
Chad Slattery © 1984. All rights reserved.

Manufactured in the United States of America. Nearly all Jossey-Bass
books, jackets, and periodicals are printed on recycled paper that contains
at least 50 percent recycled waste, including 10 percent postconsumer
waste. Many of our materials are also printed with vegetable-based inks;
during the printing process, these inks emit fewer volatile organic com-
pounds (VOCs) than petroleum-based inks. VOCs contribute to the for-
mation of smog.

CONTENTS

EDITOR'S NOTES

This volume was developed for institutional researchers as well as for college deans, department chairs, division heads, and academic affairs or educational services administrators in two- and four-year postsecondary institutions. The volume is dedicated to the more than 80,000 people who serve as department chairs in the United States. About 20,000 of them are new to the position each year, and most have had little or no formal preparation for the role.

Before fall 1992, I was a director of institutional research, assuming this position when the computerized student information system was in meltdown and enrollments were calculated by hand. I was an affirmative action officer when the university had no plan but many issues brewing, assistant dean of an academic unit undergoing major and rapid change due to new expectations for the unit and the hiring of a new dean, and assistant to a new university president. Each of these experiences was enormously challenging. None prepared me for the role of department chair, one that I assumed in September 1992. My personal and professional appreciation for the distinct and daily challenges these individuals face has increased significantly over the past several years.

I was warned that my scholarship would go on hold while I served as chair. In an effort to foil this prediction, I refocused my scholarship on the role of the department chair. I read some of the academic department chair literature and conducted a local pilot study about department chairs' information needs. The effort brought together my continuing interest in the role and functioning of institutional research and my teaching interests in academic organizations. The effort resulted in a paper presented at the 33rd Annual Forum of the Association for Institutional Research, "What Does an Academic Department Chairperson Need to Know Anyway?" (Kinnick, 1993). The paper is scheduled for future publication in the *AIR Professional File* series.

The major purpose of this volume of *New Directions for Institutional Research* parallels that of the paper: to increase the attention the institutional research community gives to the information needs of deans and department chairs. Johnson's observation made in 1976 remains every bit as true today: "Perhaps institutional research directors feel they need to service central administration to survive. On the other hand, if basic department decisions are not well informed the institution may not survive" (p. 77).

Higher education in this country is undergoing major transformation. This process will reshape and reposition in fundamental ways higher education's role in society, including articulation with elementary and secondary education, interaction with the world of work, and the development of citizen leadership. How well this transformation will take place depends in no small measure on the leadership of those who occupy the positions in the middle of our organizations, between executive officers and the faculty—those who carry titles such as dean, division head, and department chair.

Deans and department chairs are viewed here as pivotal change agents, individuals critically positioned to help support and even to lead the organizational change process that is underway. As a result of this view, except in Chapter One, relatively little attention is given in this volume to identifying information that supports the daily managerial tasks of these individuals, such as scheduling classes and managing budgets.

Instead, most of the information profiled in this volume relates to understanding changing student needs and facilitating student learning and to understanding faculty culture and redefining faculty work. Underlying the selection of chapters is the view that to survive, indeed, to thrive in the future, postsecondary institutions must become more learner-centered and must redefine the nature and balance of valued faculty work. Deans and department chairs are key players in these change processes. This volume supports the firm belief that institutional researchers have an important role to play helping deans and department chairs develop, interpret, and use information as they work to transform their academic units and, thus, our educational organizations.

Chapter One, by John Creswell and Marijane England, provides an introduction to the literature on deans and department chairs, describes information needs emerging within the current postsecondary education climate, and identifies a set of information for use by deans and chairs in their leadership and managerial roles. The chapter includes an especially rich bibliography, including references to the primary texts in the dean and chair literature, and some sources of professional development for deans and department chairs. It also serves as a resource chapter for anyone planning to develop an information system for deans and chairs or to conduct research that focuses on the work and roles of deans and chairs.

Chapters Two and Three focus on the learner and the kinds of information that can help the academic unit respond to changing student needs and facilitate the improvement of student learning. In Chapter Two, Virginia McMillan identifies information that can help to assess and monitor changing student needs. Information needed about both current and future students is identified. The emphasis here is on the need to disaggregate the data to the academic unit level and to help deans and chairs interpret the numbers. She argues that reports and numbers alone are insufficient. Many examples are offered of how various kinds of information can be used meaningfully.

Chapter Three, by Karen Gentemann, James Fletcher, and David Potter, is intended to support the effort to redirect higher education institutions into becoming learning-centered communities. The authors propose an academic program review process that focuses on student learning and its assessment. The assessment process is proposed as part of ongoing curricular reform. These authors argue that data alone are not enough and that institutional researchers have a major role to play in ensuring data integrity and the appropriate interpretation and use of the data.

Chapters Four, Five, and Six shift to a focus on faculty culture and faculty work. Chapter Four serves as an introduction to the constructs of and literature on faculty culture and climate and describes in practical terms how faculty culture and climate can be assessed. The academic department, with its own faculty culture, is viewed by Ann Austin as the site of intersection of four other kinds of faculty culture. This intersection can result in conflicts, tensions, and trade-offs. She argues that cultural understanding is essential to a successful change process. Roles for institutional researchers as well as for deans and chairs in assessing faculty culture are described.

Chapters Five and Six are companion chapters focused on defining, assigning, and assessing faculty work. In Chapter Five, Peter Gray and Robert Diamond propose a process and describe a set of supporting information that can be used to redefine faculty work at both the institutional and academic unit levels. They agree with Ann Austin that pressure is mounting to change faculty culture. They argue that the place to begin is in redefining faculty work. Institutional researchers become members of teams that work together as part of a planned change process, providing multiple forms and sources of information. The result is a new mission statement for the institution in which faculty work is defined.

Chapter Six, the collective effort of Peter Gray, Bronwyn Adam, Robert Froh, and Barbara Yonai, advocates the professional portfolio as a vehicle for use with assigning and assessing faculty work. The authors describe and critique the current process by which entrepreneurial individual faculty members negotiate with their unit heads over elements of their workload. The authors call for a new process, one that involves a unitwide, public, collaborative process. Institutional researchers are asked to join campus leadership teams to help develop model work assignment and assessment processes that ensure that information collection procedures are reliable and valid. They are also asked to conduct a meta-review of decisions within and across units to ensure fairness and to assess the extent to which the goals of the academic unit and of the institution have been achieved.

In Chapter Seven, I identify and discuss several implications for the work of the institutional research professional. Drawing on the work of the volume authors, I identify six themes that have implications for the role of the institutional researcher in providing useful information to deans and chairs: assessing local needs, ensuring data integrity and interpreting information, working collaboratively, expanding their own skill and knowledge bases, expanding their role in training and development, and establishing academic collegiality. The view emerges that institutional researchers increasingly must work as part of campus leadership teams, understand organizational change processes, and become engaged in activities designed to increase dean and chair understanding of students, student learning, and faculty culture. They must play a larger role in articulating the meaning of information and demonstrating how it can be used. Though still important, the provision of technical information in reports and printouts is not sufficient.

I would like to extend my heartfelt thanks to all of the volume authors for the efforts they have made. I am honored to serve as the editor of this volume. Despite being overextended professionally (all of you are doing so much), needing to respond to unanticipated local emergencies, and being hassled to revise early versions of the chapters, all of you kept going and have come through. My hope is that our volume plays a significant part in increasing the attention institutional research professionals give to the information needs of deans and department chairs.

Mary K. Kinnick
Editor

References

Johnson, F. C. "Data Requirements for Academic Departments." In J. C. Smart and J. R. Montgomery (eds.), *Examining Departmental Management*. New Directions for Institutional Research, no. 10. San Francisco: Jossey-Bass, 1976.

Kinnick, M. K. "What Does an Academic Department Chairperson Need to Know Anyway?" Contributed paper presentation at the 33rd annual forum of the Association for Institutional Research, Chicago, May 18, 1993.

MARY K. KINNICK is professor of education and chair, Department of Educational Policy, Foundations, and Administrative Studies in the School of Education, Portland State University, Portland, Oregon.

An introduction to the dean and chair literature is provided along with an information taxonomy for use with local assessments of the information needs of deans and department chairs.

Improving Informational Resources for Academic Deans and Chairpersons

John W. Creswell, Marijane E. England

In the current climate of postsecondary education, public outcries for account-ability and assessment of student learning resound in the halls of colleges and academic departments. At the same time, academic leaders of these units, chairs and deans, also face pressures to reduce budgets, adjust for a changing faculty workforce, respond to sensitive student issues, and assume greater responsibilities for being proactive leaders. Without question, college deans and academic department chairs find themselves in pivotal positions to respond to these contextual factors (Gmelch and Miskin, 1993; Tucker, 1992).

This chapter focuses on the information resources needed and used by academic chairpersons and deans. As a preface to the chapters that follow, we provide a framework for thinking about information resources. This frame-work should be valuable for both beginning and experienced chairs and deans as well as those engaged in institutional research on campus. To this end, we first review the current state of knowledge about chairpersons and deans, rec-ognizing recent scholarly attention to these positions, especially in chairing academic units. This review is followed by an examination of the climate and current challenges facing chairs and deans, drawing on broad trends, now widely discussed in the postsecondary education literature. In response to these challenges, we then suggest that chairs or deans assess their information requirements and we propose a typology of categories of information, specific examples within each category, and potential sources for locating the infor-mation on campus. We then argue that these information needs vary depend-ing on the various roles assumed by chairs and deans as well as the purpose for which the information is being used. Our chapter closes by advancing spe-cific recommendations for academic leaders, institutional researchers, and peo-ple who study issues in the academy.

NEW DIRECTIONS FOR INSTITUTIONAL RESEARCH, no. 84, Winter 1994 © Jossey-Bass Publishers

Chair and Dean Literature

What information is available about academic chairs that can enhance an understanding of their information needs and uses? Midlevel chairpersons in the academy provide leadership for structural units called divisions, colloquia, or more commonly, departments (Seagren, Creswell, and Wheeler, 1993). The titles these people hold vary. They are called heads, department executive officers, or, most often, chairs or chairpersons. Approximately 80,000 individuals in our 3,500 institutions of higher education hold this position, and they turn over at a rate of about 20,000 a year (McGlone and Kovar, 1992; Norton, 1980). They serve for approximately six years and 65 percent of them return to faculty positions (Carroll, 1990).

Despite their short tenure, these people hold significant positions on campuses; an estimated 80 percent of all decisions made in the academy are enacted at the departmental level (Roach, 1976). On many campuses, chairpersons supervise daily departmental operations, are actively involved in hiring and promotion and tenure issues, and prepare budgets and long-range plans. The extent to which they embrace and have responsibility for these duties may be mediated by whether they are essentially an administrative appointee of the dean, appointed with faculty consultation, or elected by departmental faculty (Tucker and Bryan, 1991). Regardless of their official responsibilities, chairs have reported that they gain satisfaction through helping faculty grow and develop and through building and developing program areas within their unit (Creswell and others, 1990). On the negative side, chairs are often stressed by inadequate time for administrative duties, pressures to keep current in their discipline, and job demands interfering with personal time (Gmelch, 1991).

In the last fifteen years, the literature about chairing has exploded exponentially. The baseline for this growth might be Tucker's book, *Chairing the Academic Department: Leadership Among Peers,* first published in 1981. Perhaps encouraged by the popularity of this book, many authors throughout the 1980s penned doctoral dissertations, journal articles, monographs, and newsletters focused on academic chairs. Private foundations also became involved and, in 1987, the Lilly Foundation and the Teachers Insurance and Annuity Association and College Retirement Equities Fund (TIAA-CREF) sponsored a project to understand the faculty development practices of excellent chairs (Creswell and others, 1990). Soon thereafter, the Danforth Foundation and the University Council on Educational Administration funded the Center for the Study of the Department Chair at Washington State University. Also established as an initiative by Maricopa Community College, the National Chair Academy was founded for two-year chairpersons. In 1990 alone, three major books about chairpersons—by Bennett and Figuli, by Moses and Roe, and by Creswell and others—were published.

Whereas articles and books about academic chairs have saturated the market, the position of the academic dean has received little scholarly attention

From a small, growing body of literature, what do we know about academic deans? Most academic deans preside over colleges, schools, or divisions; on the community college campus, the deans may be responsible for campuswide instruction. To explore the roles and responsibilities of deans, two substantive contributions emerged in 1981, the first a book by Morris (1981) that discussed from a dean's perspective the human side of personnel management, public and student relations, budget planning, affirmative action, faculty politics, salary disputes, and tenure decisions. The second contribution was a short newsletter article by Bowker (1981) that assessed the roles and role conflicts faced by academic deans. On a larger scale, two recent books have been published by noted authors. In 1988, Tucker and Bryan issued the first edition of their comprehensive text on the academic dean (see Tucker and Bryan, 1991). In it they assessed the dean's role on a variety of internal-college and campuswide areas. In 1990, Vaughn wrote a comprehensive book about deans—this time, however, about community college deans of instruction.

Despite this small literature and aside from the Vaughn (1990) book, a national profile of the demographic characteristics of deans does not exist. Within specific types of institutions and disciplines, however, we have more information. For example, Bowker and others (1985) studied the demographic characteristics of academic deans in liberal arts colleges. From responses of 371 liberal arts academic officers representing church-related colleges, private colleges, and state colleges, Bowker found that they held their positions for an average of just under five years and had 46 different titles. In another study, McLean (1993) is examining, with funds from the Lilly Endowment the demographic characteristics of chief academic officers of 220 theological schools in the United States and Canada.

On a less empirical note, anecdotal evidence suggests that the dean's position has both satisfactions and dissatisfactions. It affords the opportunity to build, restructure, and enhance an entire college (Tucker and Bryan, 1991), offers a comprehensive view of one's campus through interactions with other administrative leaders, and provides a detailed knowledge of the diverse unit needs within the college. The dean can encourage academic excellence, contribute to collegewide curriculum development, and assist in building an excellent staff through substantial involvement in the hiring and promotion process (Bowker, 1981). On the downside, on becoming a dean one relinquishes significant control over one's calendar and time, public utterances are taken as the view of the college, and the job often entails endless mediation of conflicts between contentious factions (Tucker and Bryan, 1991).

Postsecondary Education Climate

Based on the current climate in postsecondary education, what are the issues confronting chairpersons and deans that affect their need for new and expanding information? For purposes of this discussion, the same issues are addressed for both deans and chairpersons. Because distinctions may exist in how deans and chairpersons react to the issues (because they hold positions at different levels in the campus structure), we cite specific applications for both types of positions. We identify the most salient issues based on recent discussions about academic leaders and issues (Seagren, Creswell, and Wheeler, 1993; Russell, 1992).

The issues of accountability (and assessment), resulting in lost public confidence, allegations of costliness, and the need to be responsive to external constituents have created new information demands on academic administrators (Chaffee and Sherr, 1992). One manifestation of this movement is the increased state legislation about faculty workloads now found in twenty-three states (Russell, 1992). Other signs are the increased interest in assessing the outcomes of student learning and more public discussion of the appropriate role of state-level coordinating commissions in program review and campus fiscal responsibility. These external assessment needs translate into new information needs for chairs and deans such as assessing how faculty spend their time, measuring classroom outcomes, developing summary reports for external commissions, and requiring staff to update vita for accrediting agencies. Assessment of student outcomes has also received considerable attention. Muffo (1992) conducted a study of the member institutions of the National Association for State Universities and Land Grant Colleges and reported on involvement of campuses in undergraduate student outcomes assessments.

Along with the demand for increased accountability and assessment, there has been an unprecedented public demand for increased quality in colleges and universities. Greater attention is being focused on the quality of the process, the curriculum, and the outcomes of higher education in order to meet the expectations of the students who attend institutions and the public that supports higher education and employs its graduates. Many universities and colleges are borrowing the Total Quality Management (TQM) approach from business. Chaffee and Sherr (1992) address TQM for applications within the academy.

Reduced funding and the need to reallocate funds internally have also led to new demands on chairs and deans. For state institutions, the amount of state tax appropriations for higher education declined 1.5 percent between fiscal year 1991 and 1993 (Layzell, Lovell, and Gill, 1994). With this decline, the burden of revenue generation increasingly falls on colleges and departments (Seagren, Creswell, and Wheeler, 1993). Deans are faced with retrenchment decisions such as the elimination, reduction, and reallocation of academic programs that require the use of objective data for policy decisions (Ashar and Shapiro, 1990). Chairs, on the other hand, must have up-to-date information about their programs to present alternative scenarios to deans. On the income side, deans and chairs look within their units for profit centers that generate money, whether this money comes from alumni through special fundraising programs or through new fees for laboratory classes. Chairpersons are establishing internal e-mail networks to better inform faculty about external grants and contracts. Information about the alumni, the number of laboratory classes, and opportunities for external funds (Layzell and Lyddon, 1990) becomes new data to be shared and discussed in colleges and departments.

Issues about the faculty and staff workforce extend beyond the external demands for workload information. Recruiting and retaining minorities has become a central concern of deans and chairs (Hynes, 1990). Despite the lifting of the mandatory retirement age, national faculty turnover is not as great as was expected when projections were made ten years ago. This fact has raised concerns in colleges and departments about the pool of potential retirees, the options for early retirement, whether an aging workforce is productive, and the increased use of non-tenure-track and part-time faculty (Baldwin, Chronister, Rivera, and Bailey, 1993; Gappa and Leslie, 1993). Information about the supply side of faculty hiring pools, especially among cultural minority groups, must be available for chairs and deans. Current faculty retirements must be monitored and projections made about resources needed for instruction in the short-term future.

In the student area, chairs and deans are responding to new ethical and legal issues. Charges such as academic dishonesty and sexual harassment are increasingly being brought by students before deans and chairs for arbitration (Cahn, 1990; Riggs, Murrell, and Cutting, 1993). Departmental and college committees are appointed to establish guidelines for sexual harassment. These issues place chairs and deans in a role of collecting systematic data about the quality of faculty teaching and performance and responding to complaints from parents, students, and faculty. Litigation, it seems, is increasingly at the doorstep of chairs and deans. Deans and chairs are also facing the need to accommodate students with disabilities and different learning styles as the Americans with Disabilities Act of 1990 is interpreted and institutions are faced with issues of compliance.

Finally, leadership in the academy is becoming more technical and complex, requiring a trained pool of academic administrators who possess expertise on topics as diverse as the law, budgets, and academic and professional accreditation, and who exhibit strong interpersonal skills in negotiation, persuasion, conflict resolution, and motivation. The traditional model of competent faculty being elevated to leadership roles and learning on the job is rapidly becoming outdated and counterproductive because deans and chairpersons increasingly function within the much broader context of higher education. Deans and chairs must network with their peers to learn and to negotiate transitional experiences as they make career moves from faculty to leader roles (Gmelch and Miskin, 1993). With growing popularity, workshops and conference opportunities abound for practitioners (McDade, 1987) and they are available nationally through such organizations as the American Council on Education, the Association of American Colleges and Universities, the Center for Instructional Development at Kansas State University, and at the National

Chairperson Conference in Arizona sponsored by the National Chair Academy of Maricopa Community College. Several newsletters are available, including *Academic Leader* by Magna Publishers of Madison, Wisconsin, and *The Department Chair* by Anker Publishing of Bolton, Massachusetts.

Typology of Information Needs and Uses

How do these issues and challenges affect chairs' and deans' information needs and uses? As already suggested, these challenges have already begun to shape information needs. It is therefore timely to assess what information is being collected and used by chairpersons and deans and whether the information meets their needs. This activity might begin with a map of the information terrain, one we have conceptualized building on preliminary work by Hickson, Stacks, and Scott (1992).

Hickson, Stacks, and Scott advance seven categories of information used by a chair: personnel records of faculty and staff; budget information from current and past years; departmental data on majors, graduates, alumni; advising procedures; general policies and procedures; facilities and allocations; and schedule information. They provide a list of files that chairs should build according to these categories of information.

A similar typology was advanced by a physics chair at Virginia Tech who identified six types of data that come across a department head's desk (Roper, 1993): budget (observing how different budget categories are being depleted); teaching (keeping track of enrollments, grades, and teaching assignments); students (keeping track of progress); alumni (updating alumni addresses, jobs, and gifts to the department); faculty (evaluating faculty and tracking faculty data); and space (building plans showing locations of people and equipment).

Roper (1993) believes that department chairs should use data bases to graph trends in these areas. Some department chairs have developed their own data bases, such as one illustrated by a chair interviewed by Kinnick (1993, p. 12): "This department had developed its own student data base, software to complete departmental purchase requests and record encumbrances, a way to compare budget files with dean's office budget records, a spreadsheet to track courses and teaching assignments, a system for manually entering hard copy enrollment data into its own spreadsheet for tracking and projects, a spreadsheet for calculating merit pay allocations and a spreadsheet for tracking and monitoring changes in student evaluations of instructor performance."

An approach as systematic as Roper's would undoubtedly require time, personnel, and expertise to implement. Although it may be useful to establish computer programs or processes to identify information, a beginning point for most chairs and deans would be to conceptualize the categories of information needed and used. Table 1.1 identifies nine categories of information that chairs or deans might use to assess their current information needs.

Table 1.1. Categories, Types, and Sources of Information

Categories of Information	Examples of Types of Information	Examples of Sources of Information
Personnel records of faculty and staff	Vita Dates of hire Annual evaluation reports (annual reviews, salary history, promotion) Faculty teaching evaluations	Campus human resource office Campus human resources information system Departmental files Dean's files
Budget information	Annual allocations in operating and instructional budget (salaries, equipment, supplies, travel, scholarship) Annual expenditures (same areas)	Campus business office Campus financial management system Department files Dean's files Financial aid office Development office Research office
Student records/ enrollments	Demographic data Hours completed Graduate date Alumni records (major, date of graduation, placement) Enrollment data Student learning outcomes	Campus student information system Admissions and registrar's office Faculty Institutional research office Alumni office
Student advising information	Program requirements College graduation requirements Advising loads	College catalogues Program descriptions Faculty
Policies and procedures of department, college, and institution	Faculty procedures Board policies Departmental/college policies (teaching, evaluation, governance, rank, planning calendar)	Faculty handbook Department/college operations manuals Board/college policy manuals
Facility and space information	Space available and needed Equipment inventory	Campus facilities inventory and inventory management systems Campus business office Dean's office Departmental office

(continued)

Table 1.1. *(continued)*

Categories of Information	Examples of Types of Information	Examples of Sources of Information
Scheduling information	Annual schedule of classes Classroom assignments Office assignments	College calendar schedule Dean's folder on room assignments Departmental folder on room assignments
Professional/discipline information	Dates of professional meetings New books Internet e-mail addresses Current journals	Dean's professional file Department chair's professional file National, state, and regional associations
Environmental information	Trends in community demands for programs and services Areas of potential new student enrollments Supply and demand trends for faculty Economic indicators for the campus External funding opportunities for research or teaching Campus fundraising efforts	Campus institutional research office Campus alumni office Department or college special studies Bureaus of business research

Note: This table is a modification of two tables found in Hickson, Stacks, and Scott, 1992.

Examples are provided of types of information that might go into files and sources are cited where information can be found on most campuses. Chairpersons may place more value on acquiring information about scheduling, facilities, space, and student advising, whereas deans are more interested in off-campus and total college information as they respond to many units with diverse academic orientations. Other categories contain information valuable to both chairs and deans.

In addition to the level in the academic organization, a variety of factors affect the importance and use of these categories of information (for example, whether the authority structure in the organization is more bureaucratic or collegial, the discipline's affinity toward the value of information and its quantification, the academic roles of individuals, and the purposes of the information). Because roles and purposes can be managed by leaders, they are the next focus of attention in this discussion.

Academic Roles

Academic leaders assume different roles in their academic units. These roles or behaviors emanate from the expectations of superiors and subordinates or from self-interest or personal orientation toward the job (Bragg, 1981; Seagren, Creswell, and Wheeler, 1993; Gmelch and Miskin, 1993). Moreover, these roles may shape the information needs of leaders (Johnson, 1976). Five roles are especially useful as a heuristic to conceptualize the varied aspects of leadership and to assess information needs. An individual may embrace a combination of their roles and emphasize them in practice in varying degrees.

The chair or dean may be a faculty-oriented leader. This is a leader who places a priority on the tasks of recruiting, selecting, and evaluating faculty, as well as enhancing faculty morale and professional development. For example, a chair might emphasize the faculty development role by being a provider, enabler, advocate, mentor, encourager, collaborator, or challenger (Creswell and Brown, 1992). A dean, on the other hand, might exercise a more limited role by providing resources for travel or development leaves or by encouraging campuswide faculty development activities. In development decisions such as these, personnel records, budget information, and policies and procedures become essential files for chairs and deans.

The chair or dean may play the role of a manager. This person performs maintenance functions such as preparing budgets, maintaining department or college records, assigning duties to faculty, supervising nonacademic staff, and maintaining facilities, supplies, and equipment. Both chairs and deans often engage in this role, but the chairs become advocates for their departmental budgets, for example, whereas deans must fit the funding requests into the larger picture of the college (Tucker and Bryan, 1991). Personnel records, budget information, facility and space information, and scheduling would be important files to maintain.

The chair or dean may be oriented toward being an academic leader. This person provides long-term direction and a vision for the college or department (Gmelch and Miskin, 1993). This person actively solicits ideas for the improvement of the unit, plans and evaluates curriculum development, and provides leadership for departmental meetings or collegewide dean cabinet meetings. In terms of the campus structure, chairs often communicate for their unit and faculty upward to deans; deans, in turn, communicate to central administration for their college staff. These communications may be in the form of information about policies and procedures, alumni, students, and personnel.

The chair or dean may be oriented toward his or her discipline or field of study. This role requires maintaining vitality as a teacher, keeping current in an academic discipline, and networking with professionals in the field. These are challenging activities for busy academic leaders; chairs, for example, often experience stress over trying to remain current in their discipline

(Gmelch, 1991). Deans also can enhance their disciplines by creating a climate and environment where teaching, learning, and scholarship are intertwined (Huffman, 1992). Information about the latest literature in their field, recent trends in teaching and scholarship, and knowledge about professional opportunities would be important.

The chair or dean may be externally oriented. This orientation is evident in those who seek new student markets, look for opportunities to combine academic interests with business or industrial interests, monitor external grant opportunities, search for developments outside their units that affect the departments or units, and represent the unit to off-campus constituents. In this role, the chair or dean becomes both "translator and spokesperson" (McDade, 1987, p. 14). Undoubtedly, deans would engage in this role more than chairs, but chairs are more and more often being involved in this role at the request of their deans. The information needed includes trend analyses available from campuswide offices, special studies undertaken at the department or college level, and information from off-campus groups.

Purposes for Using Information

In addition to roles department chairpersons and deans must play, the purposes for using information shapes the information needs and uses. Information can be used in four ways. The chair or dean uses information to respond to requests from students, faculty, other administrators, or board members (see Tucker and Bryan, 1991, about the relationship between deans and the president, provosts, and other deans). Academic leaders respond to requests for information about faculty workloads from legislators and statewide agencies, requiring updated personnel records as well as scheduling information. Chairs and deans also respond to internal requests to assess their space needs, such as moving units or a department to a new building. This response calls for facility information, scheduling information, and budget information.

The chair or dean uses information to monitor developments in the department or college (see Creswell and others, 1990, for discussions about the monitoring role of chairpersons). Trend analyses reveal changes in students enrollments and require student and environmental information. Changing student demographics may require a new strategy toward the curriculum, and the academic leader may establish a committee to monitor class sizes or assess curricular offerings. Student records, scheduling information, and environmental information assist this committee in advancing realistic recommendations. Also, chairs or deans often need to monitor the progress of new faculty toward meeting the promotion and tenure standards. Personnel records, policies and procedures, and professional information facilitate this activity.

The chair or dean uses information to plan for the short- and long-term future of the unit. Building a budget, of course, requires an understanding of current needs and a projection of future needs. Many information categories enter into the planning decisions for constructing an annual or biennial budget plan, especially information about students, the current and past budget, and personnel information (see Tucker and Bryan, 1991, for a discussion of how deans divide budgets among academic departments and programs). Planning for the professional growth of staff and faculty (and oneself) also presents a challenge requiring demographic information from professional associations, campus policy and procedural information, and staff personnel records.

The chair or dean uses information to make decisions related to personnel, budget, and scheduling in the unit. As noted by Dressel (1971), the data required by an academic leader often turn on the nature of the decision. Awarding salary increases, promoting or tenuring faculty, reallocating money, making faculty advising assignments, and hiring staff are but a few of the decision areas for chairs and deans. Chairs and deans require personnel information, budget records, a firm understanding of policies and procedures, and environmental information.

Summary and Recommendations

An expanding literature about chairpersons and a more limited examination of deans portray the centrality of these positions in the academy. The positions bring both satisfactions and dissatisfactions to role incumbents. In addition, new challenges from on-campus and off-campus sources lead to new information needs and uses. The climate for chairs and deans includes the increased demands for accountability and assessment, an emphasis on quality, the need to reallocate and reduce funding, changing demographics of the academic workforce, challenging student ethical and legal issues, and the need for a trained pool of academic leaders. In response, information essential for new chairs and deans includes personnel records; budget information; student records and information about student advising; policy and procedural manuals for the campus, college, and department; facility and space information; scheduling information; professional and discipline information for the leader to keep current in his or her profession; and environmental, off-campus information. These information needs and uses are affected by many factors, including the roles assigned, chosen, or assumed by chairs and deans and the purposes for which information is used in the workplace.

What implications exist for chairs, deans, academic leaders, institutional researchers, and those who study the academy? From institutional researchers, deans and chairs need immediate information. Information technology and electronic information access will become increasingly critical. Campuses are starting to develop integrated campuswide information systems that can give users instant access to material stored in central computer files. The future needs of chairs and deans lie in access to the information, and less in the ownership and self-generation of information. Chairs and deans might conceptualize the categories of information needed (see Johnson, 1976, for a procedure) and then draw on campus information technology to design the most efficient systems for data retrieval and analysis. In this system, institutional researchers become data architects to help chairs and deans access and retrieve information they need.

Institutional research provides information that supports institutional planning, policy formulation, and decision making. Institutional researchers must take a role in working with the information technology people to make sure that information needs are understood and can be met. Then, because of the massive amounts of information available, the role of an institutional research office becomes increasingly critical in objectively presenting trends, long-term projections, environmental scanning, and making comparisons among units within the institution. The role of institutional researchers as sorters of information for chairs and deans becomes important.

Because information comes from different sources, new chairs and deans must understand the information flow on their campus (Stacks and Hickson, 1992). The flow of information is upward from faculty and students to chairs or from chairs to deans. It is downward from central administration to deans and from deans to chairs as well as lateral from chair to chair or from dean to dean. For example, much budget information comes both upward from faculty and student needs in a department as well as downward from central administration and deans.

For those who study chairs and deans, the literature is beginning to move away from the general demographic profile of occupants of those positions and their specific roles and responsibilities, to examine cultural issues, gender issues, and special needs. To this end, more research is needed on the information needs of midlevel academic leaders. For example, little is known about how information is obtained and used in decision making. What do chairs and deans need? How do they use information? Do they value it? These critical questions remain unexplored territory. Questions about whether the information is accurate, delivered in a timely fashion, provided in a format that is not too detailed or voluminous, is retrievable from easily accessed sources, and is available when academic leaders need it are also relevant variables (Johnson, 1976). In addition to practical strategies, we need conceptual models drawn from sociology or social psychology that are grounded in exploratory qualitative studies (such as Bernier, 1987) or developed through qualitative causal modeling.

The information challenges facing chairs and deans will continue to evolve. Improving information resources will be a primary challenge facing the academy community. The typology presented here and the factors such as role and purpose that shape the nature of information needs are first steps toward better understanding the information resource needs of chairs and deans.

References

Ashar, H., and Shapiro, J. Z. "Are Retrenchment Decisions Rational? The Role of Information in Times of Budgetary Stress." *Journal of Higher Education,* 1990, *61* (2), 23–41.

Baldwin, R. G., Chronister, J. L., Rivera, A. E., and Bailey, T. G. "Destination Unknown: An Exploratory Study of Full-Time Faculty off the Tenure Track. *Research in Higher Education,* 1993, *34* (6), 747–761.

Bennett, J. B., and Figuli, D. J. (eds). *Enhancing Departmental Leadership: The Roles of the Chairperson.* New York: Macmillan, 1990.

Bernier, N. "The Dean as Participant Observer." *Journal of Teacher Education,* 1987, *38* (5), 17–22.

Bowker, L. H. "The Academic Dean." *Administrator's Update.* Washington, D.C.: ERIC Clearinghouse on Higher Education, 1981.

Bowker, L. H., and others. *The Administration of the Liberal Arts in American Colleges and Universities.* Indiana: Indiana University of Pennsylvania Graduate School, 1985. (ED 256 221)

Bragg, A. K. "The Socialization of Academic Department Heads: Past Patterns and Future Possibilities." Contributed paper presentation for the Association for the Study of Higher Education, Washington, D.C., 1981.

Cahn, S. M. (ed.). *Morality, Responsibility, and the University: Studies in Academic Ethics.* Philadelphia: Temple University Press, 1990.

Carroll, J. "Career Paths of Department Chairs: A National Perspective." *Research in Higher Education,* 1990, *32* (6), 669–688.

Chaffee, E. E., and Sherr, L. A. *Quality: Transforming Postsecondary Education.* ASHE-ERIC Higher Education Report no. 3. Washington, D.C.: The George Washington University School of Education and Human Development, 1992.

Creswell, J. W., and Brown, M. L. "How Chairpersons Enhance Faculty Research: A Grounded Theory Study." *The Review of Higher Education,* 1992, *16* (1), 41–62.

Creswell, J. W., and others. *The Academic Chairperson's Handbook.* Lincoln: The University of Nebraska Press, 1990.

Dressel, P. L., and Associates. *Institutional Research in the University: A Handbook.* San Francisco: Jossey-Bass, 1971.

Gappa, J. M., and Leslie, D. W. *The Invisible Faculty: Improving the Status of Part-Timers in Higher Education.* San Francisco: Jossey-Bass, 1993.

Gmelch, W. H. "The Stresses of Chairing a Department." *Department Chair,* 1991, *1* (3), 1.

Gmelch, W. H., and Miskin, V. D. *Leadership Skills for Department Chairs.* Bolton, Mass.: Anker, 1993.

Hickson, M., Stacks, D. W., and Scott, R. K. "Acquiring Information." In M. Hickson and D. W. Stacks (eds.), *Effective Communication for Academic Chairs.* Albany: State University of New York, 1992.

Huffman, J. G. "The Role of the Dean: Fostering Teaching as Scholarship in the School of Education Learning Community." Contributed paper presentation for the Annual Meeting of the American Association of Colleges for Teacher Education, San Antonio, Texas, Feb. 25–28, 1992.

Hynes, W. J. "Successful Proactive Recruiting Strategies: Quest for the Best." In J. B. Bennett and D. J. Figuli (eds.), *Enhancing Departmental Leadership.* New York: American Council on Education/Macmillan, 1990.

Johnson, F. C. "Data Requirements for Academic Departments." In J. C. Smart and J. R. Montgomery (eds.), *Examining Departmental Management.* New Directions for Institutional Research, no. 10. San Francisco: Jossey-Bass, 1976.

Kinnick, M. K. "What Does an Academic Department Chairperson Need to Know Anyway?" Contributed paper presentation for the 33rd Annual Forum of the Association for Institutional Research, Chicago, May 18, 1993.

Layzell, D. T., Lovell, C., and Gill, J. I. *Developing Faculty as an Asset in a Period of Change and Uncertainty*. Working paper prepared for the conference on Integrating Research on Faculty, American Association of Colleges and State Universities and the National Center for Educational Statistics, Department of Education, Washington, D.C., Jan. 10–11, 1994.

Layzell, D. T., and Lyddon, J. W. *Budgeting for Higher Education at the State Level: Enigma, Paradox, and Ritual*. ASHE-ERIC Higher Education Report no. 4. Washington, D.C.: George Washington University School of Education and Human Development, 1990.

McDade, S. A. *Higher Education Leadership: Enhancing Skills Through Professional Development Programs*. ASHE-ERIC Higher Education Report no. 4. Washington, D.C.: Association for the Study of Higher Education, 1987.

McGlone, E. L., and Kovar, S. K. "Being Assessed." In M. Hickson and D. W. Stacks (eds.), *Effective Communication for Academic Chairs*. Albany: State University of New York Press, 1992.

McLean, J. P. *Study of Chief Academic Officers in Theological Education*. St. Paul, Minn: St. Paul Seminary School of Divinity, University of St. Thomas, 1993.

Morris, V. C. *Deaning: Middle Management in Academe*. Urbana: University of Illinois Press, 1981.

Moses, I., and Roe, E. *Heads and Chairs: Managing Academic Departments*. St. Lucia, Australia: University of Queensland Press, 1990.

Muffo, J. A. "The Status of Student Outcomes Assessment at NASULGC Member Institutions." *Research in Higher Education*, 1992, 33 (6), 765–774.

Norton, S. *Academic Department Chair: Tasks and Responsibilities*. Tempe: Arizona State University, Department of Educational Administration and Supervision, 1980.

Riggs, R. O., Murrell, P. H., and Cutting, J. C. *Sexual Harassment in Higher Education: From Conflict to Community*. ASHE-ERIC Higher Education Report no. 2. Washington, D.C.: The George Washington University School of Education and Human Development, 1993.

Roach, J.H.L. "The Academic Department Chairperson: Roles and Responsibilities." *Educational Record*, 1976, 57 (1), 13–23.

Roper, L. D. "Departmental Management with Computers." *The Department Chair*, 1993, 3 (3), 8–9.

Russell, A. B. *Faculty Workload: State and System Perspectives*. Denver, Colo.: State Higher Education Executive Officers, 1992.

Seagren, A. T., Creswell, J. W., and Wheeler, D. W. *The Department Chair: New Roles, Responsibilities, and Challenges*. ASHE-ERIC Higher Education Report no. 1. Washington, D.C.: The George Washington University School of Education and Human Development, 1993.

Stacks, D. W., and Hickson, M. "Appendix B. Providing Information." In M. Hickson and D. W. Stacks (eds.), *Effective Communication for Academic Chairs*. Albany: State University of New York Press, 1992.

Tucker, A. *Chairing the Academic Department: Leadership Among Peers*. (3rd ed.) New York: American Council on Education/Macmillan, 1992.

Tucker, A., and Bryan, R. A. *The Academic Dean: Dove, Dragon and Diplomat*. (2nd ed.) New York: American Council on Education/Macmillan, 1991.

Vaughn, G. B. *Pathway to the Presidency: Community College Deans of Instruction*. Washington, D.C.: American Association of Community and Junior Colleges, 1990.

JOHN W. CRESWELL is professor of educational psychology at Teachers College, University of Nebraska at Lincoln.

MARIJANE E. ENGLAND is policy research and planning associate in the Office of Institutional Research and Planning, University of Nebraska at Lincoln.

Deans and department chairs need to know about their current and future students if they are to assess and monitor student needs and facilitate student learning.

Assessing and Monitoring Changing Student Needs

Virginia K. McMillan

Higher education has one primary purpose—to develop the talents of its students to their maximum capacities. This is a very difficult task unless the needs of students are known to those who serve them. Institutional researchers can help deans and department chairs develop a better working knowledge of their current and future students.

This chapter identifies a set of information that must be available at the program, department, school, or college unit level to be useful. Institutional researchers, working with deans and chairs, can help to identify, collect, and make available more disaggregated information about students that can assist with enrollment planning and analysis and with ongoing efforts to improve the curriculum and instructional practices at the unit levels.

Everyone knows that college students are eighteen to twenty-four years of age, begin their higher education experience the fall after graduating from high school, carry a course load of fifteen semester credit hours, live in a dormitory with their youthful peers, party on weekends, and, if geographically close enough, go home to visit their parents when their clothing needs to be laundered. Right? This may describe the student population in a few higher education institutions across the country, but it is becoming increasingly difficult to find institutions whose students fit this description. In recent decades, postsecondary education has become more accessible to all segments of the population (U.S. Department of Education, 1993b). Low-cost institutions and financial aid programs have attracted many students who otherwise would find it difficult to finance a college education. Higher education enrollments increased 41 percent between 1970 and 1980 and another 20 percent between 1980 and 1992. Much of the growth was in part-time, female, minority, and older student enrollment as well as enrollment of students with disabilities. In fall of 1991, 44 percent of the higher education population were attending part-time, 55 percent were women, 23.5 percent were racial and ethnic minorities, and 42 percent of those whose ages were known were over the age of 25. The latest figures on students with disabilities (fall 1986) indicated that 10.5 percent of the higher education enrollment reported one or more disabling conditions.

Unfortunately, the public, legislators, and even those intimately involved in higher education policy making and delivery continue to conceptualize students in the traditional mode. Teaching methods are still applied as if this were the case, and departmental planning and scheduling, by and large, are based on this premise. Only by realizing that diversity in the student population is increasing and that student needs are as diverse as their characteristics can higher education meet those needs effectively.

Samuel Johnson once said, "Knowledge is of two kinds; we know a subject ourselves, or we know where we can find information upon it." Traditionally in higher education, departmental knowledge bases lie primarily within academic disciplines with little awareness of the composition of students and the impact that composition has on learning. Institutional researchers, on the other hand, probably are more aware of the composition of their institution's student body than anyone else on campus. In the past, however, all too often the use of this information has culminated in reports to state and federal agencies or, at most, in an institutional databook that administrators may, but probably do not, use for examining how their college or university is faring.

Until recently, few institutional research offices had taken the next step—providing information and identifying the implications of this information to those in the trenches. The presentation of data at these disaggregated levels, however, is not enough. Information is also needed about the implications of the data. Analogous to the old saying, "I gave them books and gave them books, and still they can't read," institutional researchers have a tendency to "give them reports and give them reports, and still they don't change."

Information is becoming increasingly available to the end user, deans and chairs, through direct access to computer data bases. Within this environment, the role of the institutional researcher becomes one of assisting data users to go beyond the numbers themselves to the meaning of the numbers. To remain effective, institutional researchers must increase their support of deans and chairs in professional development activities. Increasingly, institutional researchers must work collaboratively with division and department deans and chairs to identify and develop the needed information.

This chapter is divided into two sections, one dealing with information regarding current students and the other with future students. Types of information, sources of information, and how this information can be used effectively at the departmental or division level are discussed. Table 2.1 provides an overview of the potential types of data, whether the sources of data are internally or externally available, and whether they have implications for current or future students.

Table 2.1. Changing Student Needs: Information for Deans
and Department Chairs

	Data Sources		Students	
Data Set	Internal	External	Current	Future
Race or ethnicity	X	X	X	X
Gender	X	X	X	X
Age	X	X	X	X
Educational experience	X		X	
Work and community experience	X		X	
Attendance patterns	X		X	
Centrality	X		X	
Course retention	X		X	
Program retention	X		X	
Graduation rates				
Persistence rates				
Employment rates		X	X	X
Transfer rates		X	X	X
Transfer success		X	X	X
Employer evaluation		X	X	X
Job market		X	X	X

Knowing Current Students and Their Needs

Deans and department chairs face a myriad of problems and issues as they address the day-to-day and future operations of their departments. They play that critical role of serving as the intermediary between students, faculty, and institutional administration. They must not only ensure that the needs of the students in their programs are being met, but increasingly must also demonstrate that those needs are being met through effective and efficient operation of their programs. The role of the institutional researcher is to help deans and chairs identify and use information that can assist them in developing programs and policies that effectively support student needs.

Many factors, such as multiculturalism, age, gender, general aptitude, educational experience, work experience, current employment, attendance patterns, financial need, commuter versus residential status, and definition of goals influence student needs. Although educators may not be able to influence many of these factors, they can enhance efforts to serve students better by knowing what these factors are and what impact the factors have on students' abilities to learn. Enhanced student achievement and persistence, departmental productivity, faculty satisfaction, and overall institutional effectiveness can result from these efforts.

Most of the descriptive information on demographic factors such as age, gender, race, and ethnicity is available from most institutional student data bases. All too often, however, it is not readily available by department or division for use by chairs and division deans. Student characteristics and goals can differ significantly among departments or divisions. Management information systems should be structured to provide data reports, both printed and electronic, by division, department, and program. Department personnel must be aware of what students bring with them to the institution, followed by what happens to them while they are at the institution, and finally what happens to them after they leave the institution.

The increasing diversity of the student population presents challenges. As Daryl Smith (1992) points out, the focus of diversity analysis is turning away from background characteristics of students toward factors affecting success. Are the department and the programs in the department serving a representative distribution of diverse students? If not, why not? If so, are there differences in the retention and graduation patterns and learning outcomes among the various groups within the department? Institutional researchers should, at minimum, examine the following set of student characteristics with department chairs/deans.

Multiculturalism. The concept of multiculturalism involves the distribution and the importance of American-born racial and ethnic minority students and students from other countries in our colleges and universities. According to the latest national statistics (U.S. Department of Education, 1993a), 1991 higher education minority and nonresident alien student enrollment reached nearly 3.4 million, an increase of 76.4 percent since 1976. The nearly 3 million minority students now make up more than 21 percent of total enrollment in higher education institutions, compared to 15.7 percent in 1976.

Colleges and universities also enrolled 416,400 nonresident alien students in fall 1991, an increase of 90 percent since 1976. These latter figures may be considerably undercounted because there are indications that nonresident alien populations are underreported in state and national statistics.

Increases in minority and foreign enrollments cross all sectors of higher education regardless of type of institution. Departments must examine the racial and ethnic distribution of their student populations to determine who they are serving and how that distribution has changed over time. They need comparative data for the institution as a whole and for other departments within the institution. Likewise, data on peer group departments from other institutions is helpful not only in determining whether recruitment efforts should be enhanced but also in identifying colleagues who may be able to assist in developing successful recruitment, retention, and graduation strategies. Most state departments of higher education can provide comparative data by program. If the data are not readily available through existing administrative data bases, institutional researchers should assist departments in establishing cooperative linkages with peer groups to share information on a regular basis.

For institutions serving large numbers from their local communities and high schools, comparative profiles of high school graduates and the community are useful for demonstrating whether programs reflect these patterns.

Census data can be aggregated from the track level up to give comparative geographical data. Information on high school graduates can be obtained from local school districts or from the state board of education.

Institutional researchers must work with deans and department chairs as they establish goals for multiculturalism and develop mechanisms to measure whether those goals are being met and if not, why not.

The following is an example of how information can be used to address issues as they arise. One institution recently determined that the faculty and administrative personnel in departments with a major influx of immigrant students had very little understanding of the cultural background from which the students came. Their traditional mode of interaction with students was not producing positive reactions from these new students. Professional development seminars were initiated, resulting in a greater understanding of the verbal and nonverbal communication nuances related to the cultural backgrounds of their new students. Peer student mentors, assigned to new students, helped identify problems and communicate these to faculty and departmental personnel.

Gender. Is the department serving a representative proportion of males and females? If not, why not? Is there a difference in performance, retention, and program completion based on gender of the student? If so, are there conditions within the department that contribute to underrepresentation or outcome differences? Women played a major role in the increase in higher education enrollment between 1979 and 1992 (U.S. Department of Education, 1993c). During this time period, female enrollment grew by 34 percent, nearly twice the growth rate of male enrollment. The increases have occurred at all levels of higher education. Although women now represent 54 percent of the total higher education enrollment, only 39 percent of all professional program students are female. Likewise, underrepresentation of males or females occurs in many major fields of study regardless of the level of student.

As was the case with multiculturalism, historical and current student gender data are available on most institutional data bases. Information from these data bases, along with comparative data from external sources, can help departments establish baselines and benchmarks.

Age. As with race, ethnicity, and gender, the age structure within higher education is changing. The number of older students has been growing more rapidly than the number of younger students (U.S. Department of Education, 1993b). Between 1980 and 1990, the number of students under age twenty-five increased by 3 percent. During the same period, enrollment of students age twenty-five and over rose by 34 percent. The National Center for Education Statistics projects that enrollment of students over age twenty-five will rise by 14 percent between 1990 and 1998 whereas the number of students under age twenty-five will increase only by 6 percent. The largest increases will occur in the thirty-five and older age group. In 1990, this group made up 18.7 percent of the higher education population. By the year 2004, this age group is projected to make up nearly 21 percent of enrollments (U.S. Department of Education, 1993c).

These changes have had and will continue to have a significant impact on college programs. Pappas and Loring (1985, p. 138) point out that "colleges and universities now seem willing to educate the adult; but they are at the same time unsure of how to respond to the adult student's needs." Marienau and Chickering (1982, p. 5) indicate that "[r]elatively few colleges and universities are fully responsive to diverse adult learners." This statement is as true now as it was twelve years ago. Adult learners are extremely diverse. They bring a myriad of life experiences and complex needs with them.

Changes in age structure also raise some interesting research questions at the program level. It is not enough to simply examine an age profile. Institutional researchers must work with departments to determine the relationships between age and degree completion, time to degree, enrollment patterns, and characteristics of the educational experience. Grosset (1991), using discriminant function analysis, provides a model for examining multivariate differences in short-term persistence and nonpersistence for older and younger students that can be expanded to examine other variables and their relationship to age.

Many of these older students have not been in an academic environment for several years. Initially, they may doubt their ability to handle academic work successfully. Just as colleges and universities may develop support services such as child care and workshops, departments can help facilitate a smooth transition for returning students by forming support groups within their departments. In addition, if the data demonstrate an older population of students, offering evening and weekend classes should be considered.

Work and Community Experiences. Closely related to age are students' work and community experiences. What knowledge and skills do students bring to the classroom, as well as to programs and departments? Few colleges and universities routinely collect this kind of information on admission applications or registration forms. However, these factors can have a major impact on students' attitudes toward their learning experiences.

Departments should consider collecting this kind of information on their students. Students' experiences can be a valuable resource to the department or division. Students may well have gained relevant knowledge and skills from past experiences that faculty value and need but do not possess. A department may want to involve these students as guest lecturers, in faculty development activities, in faculty research and service projects, and as teaching or research assistants.

As faculty take the time to learn more about their students, the students feel more validated as learners and as whole persons. This can be especially important with adult students. Often, older students have jobs, families, and other responsibilities and associations outside the institutional community. Unlike younger students who join student organizations and may live in dormitories, these students may come to campus only for their coursework.

Classroom experiences and interactions with faculty can have a significant effect on student commitment to their role as learners, on student retention, and on program completion (Tinto, 1993).

Educational Experience. Information about a student's previous educational experiences can assist departments in diagnosing problems that may arise with student performance in particular courses or parts of the curriculum. Within the current national and state-level context of educational reform, curriculum articulation between the public schools and postsecondary education and between community colleges and four-year colleges and universities is becoming increasingly important.

A department must know what other institutions students have attended. Recent studies using a statewide data base of Illinois public higher education students show that it is relatively common for students to attend as many as four or five colleges or universities in their pursuit of a degree. Access to shared data bases can produce valuable information by departments in a relatively easy manner. Analyses of this information can lead to valuable cooperation between faculties at various institutions.

For example, a university discovered that several students transferring from a particular community college were having difficulty with a specific upper-division course. Working with the institutional research offices at the two institutions, through transcript analysis, the department chairs learned that the students had all taken the same prerequisite course from the same instructor at the college. The faculty from the two institutions worked together to identify an area of weakness in the course syllabus. Out of this one experience, the department chairs established an ongoing cooperative program of faculty communication.

Institutional researchers, working with deans, department chairs and registrars, are in a position to assist with the development of these data bases. Several states, including Florida, Colorado, Minnesota, Illinois, Virginia, and Washington, have created statewide unit record data bases. Others, such as Missouri and Oregon, are in the developmental stages of data base creation. Care should be taken to ensure that policies on the establishment of the data bases and release of the data adhere to national and state confidentiality laws. A recent report by the National Forum on Education Statistics (U.S. Department of Education, 1994) presents the results of two studies. *Compilation of Statutes, Laws, and Regulations Related to the Confidentiality of Education Data* contains a survey, abstract, and analysis of federal and state restrictions and stipulations regarding data confidentiality issues. The second study in the report, *Education Data Confidentiality and Access,* covers major court challenges, data collection issues germane to education, and trends expected to affect data confidentiality policy.

Attendance Patterns. In the early 1970s, approximately one-third of the students enrolled in higher education attended on a part-time basis (U.S. Department of Education, 1993b). Today, that proportion has risen to more than 44 percent. This distribution is projected to remain relatively stable through the year 2004 (U.S. Department of Education, 1993c). Attendance status varies considerably by type of institution. For example, in 1991, part-time students made up 65.1 percent of the public two-year college enrollment and 30.3 percent of the students attending private four-year institutions. Attendance patterns can be just as varied among departments within an institution.

Knowledge of students' planned attendance patterns can become a factor in determining course scheduling. Obtaining required courses that are not taught every term can become especially problematic for part-time students, increasing time to completion by as much as a year or more and increasing their costs. Institutional researchers can assist chairs and deans in developing and analyzing short survey forms designed to provide this kind of information as input to course planning activities.

Centrality. Programs serve different clientele in varying degrees. In this age of accountability and renewed emphasis on productivity, many departments are being asked to examine their programs in light of the overall college or university mission. A component of this examination is reviewing the extent to which programs serve students who are not program majors. Within small specialized departments, obtaining this information may not be a problem. In larger departments such as business, the need for access to the information from computer analyses is greater. Although a program may have a small number of majors, the courses may serve other programs or meet general education requirements. On the other hand, a program could be a candidate for discontinuation if it is costly and serves only a small number of its own majors.

Knowing Future Students and Their Needs

In addition to assisting departments and divisions with information and research on current student populations, institutional research offices can provide assistance to departments and divisions as they plan for the needs of their future students. Although awareness of changes in demographic characteristics described in this chapter provides insights into future enrollments, speculation on the needs of future student populations can be accomplished, in part, by knowing what has happened to former students and what their views are of their educational experience. How do employers evaluate programs based on their experience with former students? What are employers' perceptions of their future needs? What is the future job market for graduates? Answers to these questions are essential to assess changes in curricular and support service needs and to estimate future program demand and enrollment patterns.

Employment and Continued Education. Depending on the type of programs offered within a department, the employment of former students may be a critical piece of information. Former student employment information can help to assess the effectiveness of programs as well as provide insights into needed future directions. Changes in the type of jobs graduates are obtaining and the skills required to successfully perform the job responsibilities can help identify emerging specialty areas that will attract new markets.

The most common method of obtaining employment information is follow-up studies. An extensive review of the use of follow-up studies is provided by Melchiori (1988). Suskie (1992) offers a guide to the basic steps of survey research, which can serve as a useful reference tool for conducting follow-up surveys. More recently, however, basic employment information is being obtained from state administrative employment records. Stevens (1989a, 1989b, 1991) has written extensively about the use of state unemployment insurance records for obtaining employment and wage information.

A number of states (including Illinois, Texas, and Washington) have established employment tracking systems that match student identification (social security) numbers with state employment files. Although there are some limitations to the data, this process can provide information on where a former student is employed by Standard Industrial Classification (SIC) code and name and address of the employer, quarterly wages, unemployment information, and whether the former student is seeking a job through the state employment service. Employment records also can be tracked over time to determine job retention and wage advancement. In most states, these systems cannot provide information on the student's occupation, and the wage information is limited in that total earnings are reported by quarter. Self-employed and government workers are not covered by the system. Despite these drawbacks, valuable insights can be gleaned from the available information. Some states are piloting projects to share their data bases so that out-of-state employment also can be tracked.

The data obtained from these systems can be organized by program code (CIP) and provided to departments as a measure of the successful employment outcome of former students. An additional use of the data is the identification of employers for departmental or programmatic advisory groups to strengthen programs and identify future program emphases.

As important as information on employment is the knowledge of whether students are continuing their education following their departure from the program. These data are important particularly for community college programs that are preparing students for transfer and for baccalaureate programs with substantial numbers pursuing graduate education. Again, until recently, obtaining this type of information was problematic. States such as Florida and Illinois have established higher education unit record data bases that contain information on all students enrolled in or graduating from higher education institutions. These data bases are extremely useful in identifying trends in transfer patterns that can be used in departmental planning. Information from the data bases can be organized by fields of study at both the sending and receiving institution.

Where tracking systems are not available or where additional information is desired, colleges and universities are supplementing employment and education tracking system information with follow-up surveys. These surveys can provide additional information on job positions, transfer academic majors, and student satisfaction. Often, a standardized statewide or institutional survey instrument is used. However, a department may want specific information on its students that can be appended to the standardized instrument. Results of the survey should be provided to the department along with comparative data for the institution or state as a whole and for similar programs at other locations. Dillman (1978) and Suskie (1992) are only two of the many excellent resource books on survey research and displaying the results in a user-friendly manner.

Employer Evaluation. Employers can be a valuable resource for identifying program strengths and weaknesses and the direction curricula should take in the future. The traditional method used to obtain information from employers has been to first survey graduates and then survey employers of these graduates with a short mailed or telephone survey instrument rating graduates on such variables as technical skills, basic skills, and general satisfaction with the employees' performance (Banta, 1993). Although the results of these surveys generally are very positive and make good public relations material, they rarely provide substantive information needed by departments.

Better information on specific strengths and weaknesses in the curriculum and potential future markets can be gleaned from focus group discussions. Institutional researchers can assist a department and its faculty in designing focus group sessions and framing the questions that will stimulate meaningful responses and discussion. If done properly, everyone involved benefits—the institution gains support from business and industry, the department improves its programs' curricula, the institutional research office establishes working relationships with departments, and, most importantly, students get a better education. Morgan (1993) and Krueger (1994) provide useful information on the use of focus groups.

Job Market. One of the most perplexing tasks facing a dean or department chair is projecting the demand for a program. Although the projections for the nation, state, type of institution, and institution give a general direction that enrollments will take, program enrollments are more often driven by the job market. A wealth of labor market information exists. In the late 1970s, Congress established the National Occupational Information Coordinating Committee and specified that each state should establish similar committees. These committees, representing education, labor, economic development, and other agencies, are charged with coordinating and disseminating labor market and career information. Methodologies for projecting employment demand have improved over the past few years, and these data along with supply data from educational institutions are available in computerized occupational information systems generally grouped by clusters of occupations and educational programs. Most of these systems have been expanded to include supplemental information such as wages and interpretive, narrative discussions of factors affecting a particular program area. This information, along with that obtained from and about former students, employers, and general enrollment projections can provide insights into future enrollments by program area. Institutional research offices should be prepared to help gather the information and assist departmental personnel in using it.

Conclusion

The role of the institutional research office in forming partnerships with academic departments and divisions will become increasingly important as higher education changes its fundamental ways of operating. Scarce resources and demands for accountability and productivity will continue to force institutions to look more closely at the internal operations of the college or university. Examination of individual departments as a part of the overall evaluation of institutional effectiveness will become the rule rather than the exception. Information on who is being served, who should be served, and who are the potential students become critical components of departmental assessment and planning.

References

Banta, T. W. *Critique of a Method for Surveying Employers.* Association for Institutional Research Professional File no. 46. Tallahassee, Fla.: Association for Institutional Research, 1993.

Dillman, D. A. *Mail and Telephone Surveys: The Total Design Method.* New York: Wiley, 1978.

Grosset, J. M. "Patterns of Integration, Commitment, and Student Characteristics and Retention Among Younger and Older Students." *Research in Higher Education,* 1991, *32* (2), 159–177.

Krueger, R. A. *Focus Groups: A Practical Guide for Applied Research.* (2nd ed.) Newbury Park, Calif.: Sage, 1994.

Marienau, C., and Chickering, A. W. "Adult Development and Learning." In B. Menson (ed.), *Building on Experiences in Adult Development.* New Directions for Experiential Learning, no. 16. San Francisco: Jossey-Bass, 1982.

Melchiori, G. S. (ed.). *Alumni Research: Methods and Applications.* New Directions for Institutional Research, no. 60. San Francisco: Jossey-Bass, 1988.

Morgan, D. L. *Successful Focus Groups: Advancing the State of the Art.* Newbury Park, Calif.: Sage, 1993.

Pappas, J. P., and Loring, R. K. "Returning Learners." In L. Noel, R. Levitz, D. Saluri, and Associates (eds.), *Increasing Student Retention: Effective Programs and Practices for Reducing the Dropout Rate.* San Francisco: Jossey-Bass, 1985.

Smith, D. G. "Diversity." In M. S. Whiteley, J. D. Porter, and R. H. Fenske (eds.), *The Primer for Institutional Research.* AIR Resources for Institutional Research, no. 7. Tallahassee, Fla.: Association for Institutional Research, 1992.

Stevens, D. W. *Using State Unemployment Insurance Wage-Records Data to Construct Measures of Secondary Vocational Education Performance.* Washington, D.C.: U.S. Congress, Office of Technology Assessment, 1989a.

Stevens, D. W. *Using State Unemployment Insurance Wage-Records to Trace the Subsequent Labor Market Experiences of Vocational Education Program Leavers.* Washington, D.C.: U.S. Department of Education, National Assessment of Vocational Education, 1989b.

Stevens, D. W. *New Accountability Opportunities in Public and Private Postsecondary Occupational Education Programs.* Chapel Hill, N.C.: Research and Evaluation Associates, Inc., 1991.

Suskie, L. A. *Questionnaire Survey Research: What Works.* AIR Resources for Institutional Research, no. 6. Tallahassee, Fla.: Association for Institutional Research, 1992.

Tinto, V. *Leaving College: Rethinking the Causes and Cures of Student Attrition.* (2nd ed.) Chicago: University of Chicago Press, 1993.

U.S. Department of Education. *The Condition of Education 1993.* NCES 93–290. Washington, D.C.: U.S. Government Printing Office, 1993a.

U.S. Department of Education. *Digest of Education Statistics 1993.* NCES 93–292. Washington, D.C.: U.S. Government Printing Office, 1993b.

U.S. Department of Education. *Projections of Educational Statistics to 2004.* NCES 93–256. Washington, D.C.: U.S. Government Printing Office, 1993c.

U.S. Department of Education. *Education Data Confidentiality: Two Studies.* Washington, D.C.: U.S. Government Printing Office, 1994.

VIRGINIA K. MCMILLAN *is deputy director for policy and planning at the Illinois Community College Board.*

Assessment principles and methodologies are applied to a framework for implementing a learner-focused internal program review process.

Refocusing the Academic Program Review on Student Learning: The Role of Assessment

Karen M. Gentemann, James J. Fletcher, David L. Potter

This chapter addresses the question of how institutional researchers can use assessment to support the effort to redirect higher education institutions toward fulfilling their instruction missions by becoming learning-centered communities. The strategy we propose focuses attention on student learning by reframing a common practice in academic culture—the academic program review. By this, we mean a formal internal review of institutional programs. This chapter does not address some typical components of an academic program review that remain important to chairs and deans, such as faculty quality as measured by educational preparation or productivity documented by faculty activities reports. Instead, the chapter is limited to considerations of student learning as the focus of the academic program review process. It provides examples of data needed to support this process, some of them generated by the institutional researcher and some with the help and advice of the institutional researcher.

For the past decade, critics have attacked almost every aspect of higher education—what it does and how it does it. The common thread running through these complaints is that higher education has failed to recognize and respond to changes sweeping through American society. Initially, critics decried the neglect of both our students (Study Group on the Conditions of Excellence in American Higher Education, 1984) and the curriculum (Association of American Colleges, 1985). More recently, the swiftly rising costs of a college degree have raised questions about higher education's accountability to those who pay the bills, whether in the form of tuition, tax dollars, or federal grants and contracts, and a concern that higher education is not returning full value for the money it receives. Finally, many working within higher education

NEW DIRECTIONS FOR INSTITUTIONAL RESEARCH, no. 84, Winter 1994 © Jossey-Bass Publishers

believe that their ability to respond to contemporary problems is hampered by disciplinary fragmentation and outmoded attitudes about learning and instruction. In sum, in the words of the recent Wingspread Group report (1993, p. 1), "a dangerous mismatch exists between what Americans need from higher education and what they are getting." Academic program reviews refocused by assessment can be an important tool for colleges and universities as they attempt to address these criticisms and maintain the public trust.

In the mid 1980s, many criticisms coalesced in the assessment movement, which rapidly became the means by which state legislatures and higher education coordinating bodies sought to gain greater control over colleges and universities. The reaction to assessment on college campuses has been mixed. Usually, even within an institution, one finds varying degrees of acceptance (Fuhrmann and Gentemann, 1993; Watt and others, 1993.) For many faculty, the term *assessment* is viewed as accusatory, with the implication that "normal" faculty evaluations of students are masking poor performance. For these faculty, the fact that students are not doing well is not news, but they insist that the responsibility for this situation rests with the student, not with the faculty or the program.

For others on campus, assessment has struck a responsive chord and has shown greater staying power than many would have predicted. A major underpinning of assessment has always been a focus on students and student learning, giving primacy to the students and what they learn rather than to the faculty and what they know. This has been accomplished by adhering to basic evaluation models that identify the goals for student learning, determine appropriate measures for achievement of these goals, and feed information back into the program.

The problem with this approach is that it works only if both administration and faculty commitment are present. If they are not, assessment serves the public accountability master, which is looking for quantifiable measures of student success and fails to refocus the curriculum on student learning.

Why Academic Program Review?

In the early 1980s, the National Center for Higher Education Management Systems (NCHEMS) found that 82 percent of the institutions they surveyed employed some type of formal program review (Barak, 1985). Although not all used the same definition of program review, the study found the use of internal program reviews to be on the rise, particularly among large research universities, beginning in the early 1970s (Conrad and Wilson, 1985). Although institutional strategies for conducting program reviews vary, their legitimacy is well-established, with debate limited to the internal wrangling over the structure of the review.

Despite their legitimacy, reviews are viewed with suspicion by some faculty who perceive them as administrative impositions unrelated to their work or concerns, a bureaucratic ritual to be fulfilled, another report to be placed unused on a dean's shelf. Others view them as an opportunity to lobby for additional resources.

Administrative interest in curriculum and student learning also can elicit faculty distrust. Some faculty insist that students and the curriculum are their province and question the motives of administrative oversight, worrying that the intent is to find ways to do more with less. External pressures for accountability, particularly at the state level, have added to faculty suspicions. For example, legislative calls for studies of the curriculum and faculty workloads exacerbate these apprehensions. To the extent that the program review process reinforces these faculty concerns and remains disassociated from their perceived interests, it threatens to remain ritualistic and unable to contribute to student learning.

In recent times, the standard, predictable, internally driven program review has tended to emphasize the inputs that are marshaled to establish and maintain the program. Often included are data that are designed to emphasize the outstanding quality of the faculty, based on the evidence of where they received their degrees, their record of obtaining sponsored research support, their publications in prestigious peer-reviewed journals, and the excellent opportunities students will have to be taught by faculty knowledgeable and current in their field. Also mentioned may be faculty actions to adjust the curriculum in response to developments in the field and shifting faculty research interests.

The review may question the quality of students in the program, expressing concerns about their basic skills on entering the curriculum and perhaps citing statistics about their SAT scores, high school grade point averages, or course preparation. However, the review may generally conclude that, despite these difficulties, students do succeed. Evidence to support this conclusion may include the number of graduates who have pursued graduate studies in the field or taken jobs related to the discipline.

The standard internal review will then likely conclude with a statement that improvements can be made if sufficient additional resources are provided, including more faculty to reduce class size and enhance opportunities for faculty advising and informal interaction with students, and more graduate student assistants to work with students needing help. Resources also may be requested to ensure that faculty can remain current in the field by having additional time for research and study and travel support for attendance at professional meetings, with subsequent benefits for students and the program.

The primary focus of such reviews is the department, not the academic program, and most certainly not student learning outcomes. The information used as evidence of success tends to emphasize the resources available in the department to conduct all of its programs—ratios of faculty, graduate student assistants, and students; amounts of research grants and publications; and library holdings in the discipline. This information may be supplemented by limited measures of performance: student evaluations of teachers, scores of students pursuing academic careers based on the Graduate Record Examination, and occasional self-reported studies or anecdotal evidence about alumni. The program will be considered in the context of the discipline as the basis for its structure by delineating the categories defining the discipline, the logical and ideal relationships among those categories, the requirements intended to expose students to these elements of the field, and recent developments in the discipline resulting in adjustments to this basic structure.

Despite all these shortcomings, academic program review is familiar to faculty and at many institutions is part of the culture, even if not a beloved part. Thus, academic program review provides an opportunity for institutional researchers to take advantage of an existing procedure, infuse it with a new orientation, add the best of assessment, and support changes that emphasize student learning.

Need for Change

To accomplish this shift in emphasis, the conventional approach to academic program review must be replaced by a more self-reflective, process-based review. The Association of American Colleges (AAC), recently renamed the Association of American Colleges and Universities, has been engaged in a national effort to promote such a program review. Its multivolume publications on this issue (1991a, 1991b, 1992) establish the foundation for reform. Furthermore, its work with disciplinary professional associations gives it a potential platform for effecting change. Its approach is consistent with recent changes in the requirements of institutional self-studies for reaffirmation of accreditation developed by regional accrediting agencies and by many of the specialized accrediting bodies. It also is compatible with the best practices in academic assessment. Many of these accrediting bodies require a commitment to developing and implementing programmatic, student-oriented goals, establishing means by which to determine whether the goals have been met, and ultimately improving curriculum.

The AAC approach shifts the focus from the department to the program, including its actual operation and effect on students: "The goal of a program review should be the self-consciousness of faculty members and administrators about their educational practices so they can improve the quality of teaching and learning" (1992, p. 1). This goal cannot be achieved through preoccupations with static measures of departmental assets or with curricular structure with its planned sequence of courses. Instead, it must yield insights into how resources are used, the consequences of these uses, and the way in which students actually experience the major. It asks, for example, how majors satisfy their general education requirements. Are seniors taking introductory major courses? If so, what difference does it make in the attainment of the major? Ratcliff's (1988) research indicates that the way students sequence their courses, the actual curriculum, may have little relationship to the intended curriculum of requirements listed in the catalog.

Assessment and Academic Program Review

The reframed academic program review process has five stages: (1) development of student learning goals for each program, (2) articulation between goals and the curriculum, (3) selection and development of appropriate measures of student learning for each goal, including both direct and indirect measures, (4) collection and analyses of data documenting student achievement of these goals, and (5) feedback into the curriculum involving faculty reflection on results.

Development of Goals. What kind of academic program review can overcome the limitations of the conventional approach and meet the challenges of our times? It should begin, just as assessment does, with a statement of goals, articulated in terms of the knowledge and skills students are expected to achieve. This shifts attention from subject matter and department to students and learning. Second, it demands self-conscious reflection on how those goals are expressed within the curricular structure. The goal statement should be evaluated for its ability to address students' educational needs and to reflect current knowledge and directions of the major field.

Peterson and Hayward (1989) describe a useful way to proceed with the goal statement. They posed a question to their colleagues participating in a U.S. Department of Education project designed to develop indicators of student learning: "At graduation, what do you think your best graduates should know, think, do, believe, or value?" (p. 95) After preparing an extensive and detailed list, the following question was posed: "Assume we are members of a program review team from the . . . Southern Association of Colleges and Schools (SACS); please tell us how you would demonstrate to us that the skills and values on the list before you are being learned or acquired in your curriculum" (p. 103).

These are the basic questions asked in this model of an academic program review and they echo the questions raised by assessment. Answering these questions requires more than a report on grade distribution and more than knowing the proportion of graduates who plan to attend graduate school. It requires that programs and departments explicitly define learning outcomes, a process that forces faculty to identify the "knowledge components, cognitive skills, technical skills, and attitudes and values that should be learned by the best graduates of a program" (Peterson and Hayward, 1989, p. 94).

If the program review process uses these basic questions in guiding the self-study of the academic unit, the process of identifying learning outcomes and demonstrating to what extent these outcomes are being achieved will require several years to implement fully. However, given regional and specialized accreditation requirements, together with state expectations, most institutions may have already begun some version of this process. Whatever stage an institution finds itself in, all programs should identify learning outcomes. In a cyclical program review, year one should begin with the identification of goals, a plan of review and assessment activities for the year, and a schedule for subsequent years.

An institutional researcher skilled in writing objectives and goals is needed throughout these stages, but particularly in stages 1 and 3. Writing measurable goals is not a skill taught in most graduate programs, and faculty, for the most part, have never been trained to do this. Nonetheless, it is an essential component of a combined academic program review and assessment program because it provides the basis of what will follow.

The institutional researcher may hold workshops or meet with appropriate faculty to expedite this process, but ultimately, the faculty must remain in control of the curriculum and write the goals. Institutional researchers who have been involved in assessment activities report consistently that faculty who become engaged in goal-setting often institute reform in the curriculum based simply on the discussion of what program graduates ought to know and be able to do.

The institutional researcher who is supporting this faculty activity should be prepared to provide examples of program goals and to demonstrate how to turn broadly stated goals into student learning objectives. Faculty often misinterpret this task and write *teaching* goals, indicating material the faculty should cover in a degree program rather than student learning goals, indicating what students are expected to know or what skills they should have. Workshops, seminars, written guidelines, and one-on-one discussions all may be needed to accomplish this. Indeed, institutional researchers working with faculty report that this is an ongoing dialogue, a process rather than an event.

Articulation Between Goals and the Curriculum. The second element of a revised program review is an articulation of the goals as they are expressed through teaching and learning in the curriculum. The faculty must determine how effectively the requirements of the major enable students to pursue and achieve these goals. It is not unusual for lofty goals to be identified that are not really taught. Special attention should be given to ways in which connections are made among goals and elements of the curriculum. For instance, the perceived lack of writing skills is often lamented by faculty as something not being taught by the English faculty, decried as a skill lost to the current generation, or viewed as the result of the admissions office's failure to recruit the best students. However, examination of the curriculum for the major is often silent on writing. There may be no overall policy regarding how often students should be expected to write. An audit could reveal the use of multiple choice examinations and brief essays in place of lengthier papers.

Comparisons should be developed between statements of program goals, specific course requirements, and learning activities as reflected in analyses of course materials. The curricular structure should be assessed in terms of its carrying capacity, that is, the extent to which the available faculty resources can fulfill the need to offer the critical courses for the major in the context of other teaching demands. This assessment should reveal the extent to which faculty teaching responsibilities are distributed among the program under review and other curricula, such as general education, electives, other departmental programs, and other programs within the college or university.

Again, the institutional researcher may need to develop guidelines and train faculty in how to do this, but most faculty will feel on somewhat more familiar terrain with this activity. Reviewing syllabi to be sure the goals are addressed, at least in theory, is similar to the function all faculty perform when they develop a course or serve on a committee reviewing new course proposals.

A review of student course-taking patterns could also serve the academic program review process by tracking cohorts over time to determine the relationship between stated requirements and actual courses used to satisfy requirements. Such a study of the real curriculum will be beneficial in understanding which course-taking patterns are associated with the achievement of specific goals.

Measures of Student Learning. The third stage of the review process is at least as difficult as developing goals. The primary task in this phase of program review is to identify and adopt measures of student learning that are appropriate to the goals previously set. These include direct and indirect (from students and faculty) measures of student learning (see Table 3.1).

Direct Measures. In considering direct measures of student learning, the quandary for most faculty is whether to select a preexisting, off-the-shelf test or to develop their own measures. Furthermore, each campus must decide whether measures should be applied at an institutional level and the data disaggregated for each unit, or whether the data should be collected directly by the academic program. Institutional researchers play an important role in making the decision and in carrying it out. The following general guidelines can prove helpful in the selection and use of direct measures.

Table 3.1. Examples of Measures of Student Learning

Direct Measures	Indirect Measures
Written exams	Interviews
Embedded questions	Participant observation
Oral exams	Focus groups
Portfolio analysis	Satisfaction surveys
Papers	Reported job performance
Simulated activites	

Multiple measures should be used to increase the reliability of the results.

Both quantitative and qualitative measures should be used to increase reliability.

Trend data must be collected to ensure validity.

Comparative data, although not always readily available, provides credibility on the campus.

Behavioral measures provide direct indicators of a goal, whether it is in the form of increased numbers of students attending theater performances on campus or whether it is observing interactions among ethnic groups.

The selection of quantitative measures is fraught with peril. There are considerations of validity and reliability, of "fit" between the curriculum and the measure, and of cost, to mention just a few. Jacobi, Astin, and Ayala (1987) describe the range of issues to be considered when selecting measures. Because of the range of possibilities, the institutional researcher must provide guidance regarding the choices that can be made. Often, faculty will select a readily available test as a way to expedite the assessment process and to avoid the protracted discussions associated with other choices. The institutional researcher must be prepared to help faculty determine whether the test addresses the goals of its curriculum. Even when an off-the-shelf test is determined to be a good measure, the institutional researcher must assist the academic program in identifying and reviewing tests. Thus, the institutional researcher must be familiar with the major testing companies, the Educational Testing Service and American College Testing in particular. In addition, he or she should be aware of the Area Concentration Achievement Tests from Austin Peay College, the development of which was supported by a grant from the Fund for the Improvement of Postsecondary Education.

Because the selection of standardized instruments may be done to "avoid internal efforts to clarify key concepts or to define goal statements" (Jacobi, Astin, and Ayala, 1987, p. 26), the institutional researcher must revisit the use of these tests in programs that rely on little else. For instance, a program that gives the Major Field Achievement Test to its graduating seniors year after year must be encouraged to reflect on the benefits of the test before repeating it. Does it still inform them about student learning? Does it provide information on the learning goals they have established? Is the comparison group appropriate? Furthermore, reliance on a single test to assess learning goals is repudiated by scholars of student assessment (Pratt, Reichard, and Rogers, 1989; Jacobi, Astin, and Ayala, 1987). Multiple measures are not only more desirable from a measurement perspective but also more satisfying to the faculty because they provide multiple perspectives on student achievement.

Ultimately, although internal measures may lack the comparability of purchased tests, they can be designed to give feedback on the specific goals of the program, making them more likely to encourage the kind of curricular dialogue appropriate for a learning-centered academic program review. Faculty discussion about the items to include in a locally developed test often generate changes to the curriculum long before test results are in. A word of warning, however, regarding test construction: despite their familiarity to faculty, tests are not easily constructed. With the exception of departments of education and psychology, testing theory and principles are not well-known among faculty. The institutional researcher who has some experience with test construction can, therefore, be a valuable resource. Those with less experience in designing tests should be able to identify others with testing expertise, whether they are among the institution's faculty or at other institutions or are expert practitioners in the field.

Qualitative data are also needed. Many faculty, as well as chairs and deans, want more contextual data than is possible with quantitative measures. This can be the case for faculty in the physical sciences as well as those in the social sciences and humanities. What quantitative measures gain in precision, they may lose in explanatory power; that is, although it may be possible to generate statistically reliable data from multiple choice tests, for example, they often do not provide explanations for why students perform as they do. Qualitative data, especially when used in conjunction with quantitative measures, can help provide a context for understanding student performance. Many faculty will want to include such techniques as oral presentations or culminating research papers. These can be reviewed by faculty teams or outside evaluators. Many faculty who value this approach for its ability to generate more contextual data, however, need training or advice on how to create and use a criterion sheet for this purpose and how the criterion sheet itself reflects the established goals.

Another important distinction with which faculty have difficulty is that between evaluating individual students and using data about individual students to assess an academic program. For instance, performing arts programs have a long history of experience in evaluating individual student performance, often by means of outside experts or a team of faculty. This situation is ideal for adaptation to a program review. Usually there is a set of criteria for all reviewers to use. However, aggregating the data so that the review becomes an assessment of the program rather than an evaluation of the student is not always easily accomplished. The institutional researcher can help develop an appropriate mechanism for assessing such performances, and through professional networks, identify faculty at other institutions who have had experience with this process.

Portfolio assessment, which has seen a revival among assessment practitioners, is yet another option. Even modest versions of portfolio assessment, however, are labor-intensive. Some programs that use portfolios limit what can be included. For a discussion of portfolio assessment and a listing of institutions that are using portfolios, see Black, 1993.

The assessment center concept is a particularly appealing alternative to a paper-and-pencil test, but it too is very labor-intensive. The basic approach of an assessment center is to place the student in a simulated environment in which he or she typically engages in problem solving, critically analyzes a situation or dilemma, and designs a strategy for resolving the problem. Students can work alone or in groups, as desired. For a full discussion of this concept and the identification of institutions that are using assessment centers, see Millward (1993).

Indirect Measures. In addition to these direct measures of student learning, there are indirect measures that can be very useful as indicators of student learning. These measures are often suitable for understanding the degree of student learning across disciplines and programs. For example, nearly all academic programs have some interest in whether their graduates attend graduate school or are employed in a related field. Most programs want to know their graduates' views on the quality of their undergraduate experience, including the degree to which students feel that their programs prepared them for graduate study or employment. Although many programs keep track of their graduates, the institutional researcher can provide this support by conducting mail or telephone alumni surveys. Although most institutions do some kind of alumni follow-up, the questions asked are usually more reflective when they are done in conjunction with program reviews.

Open-ended items can be asked that need not be coded in order to prepare disaggregated reports. One page of an alumni survey can be designed as a tear-out page to be sent directly to the department. Thus, for example, the graduate can identify the best faculty by name, provide their recommendations for program improvement, and express other thoughts about their program without the institutional researcher having to precode the information, thereby losing some of the richness of the data.

Many other studies provide the institutional researcher with opportunities for collecting information that can be easily disaggregated. Graduating senior surveys are particularly easy because they can be distributed through the departments, reducing costs and, with proper encouragement, increasing response rates. Retention studies can be conducted for programs in their reporting year, although these require some negotiation with deans, chairs, and program faculty about which students will be tracked. Some programs have a greater interest in time-to-graduation; others want to know retention rates for their majors. In any case, the capabilities of the student information system will be paramount in determining which type of study will be conducted.

Qualitative data involving observations or focus groups (Morgan, 1988) also can be a source of information regarding student learning. Observational data can be collected on student–student and student–faculty interactions to determine the character of the learning community. Student participant–observers can be trained to collect these data. Focus groups can also be used to learn more about student experiences with faculty, other students, and curricular requirements. Angelo and Cross (1993) have a very useful resource book on in-class assessments.

Central to a learner-based academic program review is the development and maintenance of a student data base, which typically contains the information

Table 3.2. Student Data Base

Entering Students	Continuing Students
Educational expectations and goals	Experience of campus including satisfaction
Work expectations while enrolled	with courses and campus life
Career goals	Levels of interaction with faculty
Reasons for selecting the college	Plans to change major and why
Expectations for completing a degree	Hours spent working
from the institution	Commitment to completing a degree
Anticipated sources of income while	Reasons for stopping out before graduation
enrolled	
Intended major	

Graduates	Nonreturning Students
Work experience and its relationship to	Reasons for leaving, by major
degree	Future educational plans
Postbaccalaureate education experience	Suggestions and recommendations for
Reflections on the quality of degree	improvement of programs
program and educational experience	Proportion who transfer and why
Suggestions and recommendations for	
improvement of programs	

identified in Table 3.2. This, of course, is in addition to the admissions, enrollment, and graduation files with which institutional researchers usually work. For a related discussion of assessment-related student data base development, see Astin (1993).

In addition to the direct and indirect measures of student learning, studies of the faculty and the curriculum itself can be integral to an understanding of student learning outcomes. Many of these will be conducted by the faculty themselves, often with the assistance of the institutional researcher. Others can be done by the institutional researcher in cooperation with the faculty. For example, peer evaluations of teaching can provide first-hand knowledge of how faculty transform requirements into practice. Focus groups of faculty can be particularly enriching if the focus is targeted on behavioral indicators of student learning rather than on resources, personnel, or the quality of students. A focus group led by a skilled leader (many of whom are found on our campuses) can direct these sessions into curricular discussions.

Data Collection and Analysis. The institutional researcher is a resource and a support in the academic program review process and should serve that function with regard to data collection and analysis. There are some sources of data that the institutional researcher is better equipped to collect, such as alumni or graduating senior surveys, or facilitating focus groups. However, the primary responsibility for data collection, and particularly for analysis, must remain with the faculty. Otherwise, the tendency will be for findings, as prepared by the institutional research office, to be passed on to the dean without serious review at the program level. The institutional researcher may assist the dean in developing guidelines for data analysis, which the faculty will use in preparing their reports, but the ultimate responsibility for analysis and interpretation lies with faculty.

Feedback. The fifth and final stage is that of providing feedback. Because the ultimate goal of this entire academic program review effort is to improve student learning, the collection of data cannot become an end in itself, nor can it simply be reported to the dean without formal reflection on the part of the faculty about the meaning of the data. The institutional researcher should play an active part in interpreting the findings and explaining the limits of the methodology; ultimately, however, the faculty must determine the import of the data.

The program faculty must review the accumulated data, determine what in the curriculum should be changed (if anything), and design a plan of action for the improvement. Plans should be made to collect new data to determine the extent to which any program changes affect student learning. Requests for additional resources tend to emerge at this point. The program director or department head may be asked to prepare two plans of action, one based on an assumption of no additional resources and the other identifying priorities for using additional funds.

Impact on Curricular Reform

Conceptualizing the academic program review as a process that is learning-centered and uses student-based information to determine success expands the context within which the curriculum is established, revised, and implemented. The locus of the curriculum becomes the students' performances, not simply the disciplinary structure. Competence is no longer defined as success in a set of separate course experiences. Rather, competence is redefined within a broader arena of subject matter mastery involving complex processes of learning, analysis, and synthesis measured over time by a portfolio of achievements. This approach places a premium on general skills, demonstrated results, and learning milestones. Along with appropriate classroom practices and extracurricular activities, it encourages students to be active learners.

Although the activities described here may be buttressed by state or regional mandates to assess undergraduate education, the academic program review process with this orientation has even greater potential for improving programs. Academic administrators will have information on which to base more informed resource allocation decisions and faculty will have information on which to base more informed curricular decisions. Conrad and Wilson (1985) provide a full discussion of why these processes of resource allocation and program improvement should be kept distinct.

Done well, this program review approach increases the prospect that departments will take the process seriously and seek the support of the institutional research office to ensure suitable data collection procedures. To be effective, however, the institutional research office must be proactive and offer assistance at every stage of the self-study process. This is not to suggest that the institutional researcher take on the responsibilities of the department, but the institutional researcher who is well-versed in assessment practices can provide guidance as well as appropriate research support for many of the program review requirements.

The academic program review offers opportunities for the institutional researcher to be an active participant in the curricular improvement movement in which higher education is engaged. This participation requires new skills, advance preparation, and a commitment to the goals of curricular improvement, but the rewards are many. Institutional researchers are able to add to their skills and become integral players in the academic program review process.

Implications

Implementing an academic program review focused on student learning has several implications for institutional researchers as well as for deans and department chairs, who are the primary decision makers in this process. First, the data required for the academic program review based on student learning must be at the major program level as well as the department level. Thus, the assessment of learning outcomes must also be at the major program level. This magnifies the effort required for the review and means that the institutional researcher must be able to identify students by major program in institutional data bases.

Second, student-oriented data of the type discussed here are not always readily available. The program review requires the systematic collection of data over time. Only a few institutions will have these data readily available. However, because of regional accrediting standards, many institutions have begun this process and will be able to address program review issues with at least some relevant and appropriate data.

Third, an expanded definition of institutional research skills is called for if the institutional researcher is to carry out the diverse responsibilities suggested here. Quantitative skills alone have never been sufficient for an institutional researcher's multiple responsibilities, and they will not suffice in this expanded version of the job. As always, managerial skills are necessary to plan the tasks necessary to carry out this review. In addition, qualitative research skills, which have become more prominent in the institutional research literature and more frequently discussed at national, regional, and state meetings, are demanded.

Faculty have rarely been schooled in the process of developing behavioral student goals, developing a curriculum derived from such goals, or designing valid and reliable assessment techniques. An institutional researcher with this background can be invaluable to academic units struggling with these challenges. Furthermore, many departments that are engaged in the review process feel compelled to come up with numbers as indicators of their achievements. They often are not sure which qualitative data are appropriate. Clarification of these issues is incumbent on the institutional researcher, who at least is aware of the qualitative evaluation literature if not formally trained in it. The academic program review process often will rely on survey and focus group interview methodologies. If the institutional research office is not already adept at these skills, the institutional researcher who expects to be an active participant in the review process will find it important to develop them either through reading or workshops and presentations available through professional associations.

Fourth, advance planning is essential for even a modified and basic version of a program review. Much of the data must be collected long before the formal self-study is begun. The proactive institutional researcher will be ahead of the curve if he or she initiates appropriate studies.

Fifth, an assessment-based academic program review moves the student-focused curriculum improvement agenda toward a greater sense of partnership among institutional researchers, administrators, and faculty. The responsibilities inherent in this approach require a team effort, in part because no one individual has the array of quantitative and qualitative research and managerial skills needed to carry out the review. Also, the focus on student learning is premised on the concept of the campus as a learning community in which faculty, staff, and students collaborate. This orientation provides an opportunity for institutional researchers to move beyond the report-writing mentality and become full participants in curricular improvement.

Recommendations for Institutional Researchers

The institutional researcher who undertakes the task of supporting an institutional movement toward linking assessment efforts with academic program review faces both political and technical challenges.

The political reality is that whereas academic program review may be familiar to faculty, a student-learning focus is not, and resistance to this approach may be apparent in the form of hostility at one extreme or indifference on the other. Not all deans will welcome this approach either. Many faculty, in particular, will see this as interference or as a way of evaluating *them* and will not support change for what they envision as a dubious outcome. If there is an absence of broad institutional support, the institutional researcher must show examples of success or persuade one dean to "experiment" with a select program to conduct a student-centered academic program review. It is easiest to begin with an applied program, preferably one that is accredited by an outside agency. These programs, for the most part, are already conducting student-focused accreditation reviews and could most easily adapt an internal review along the same lines.

Technical competence must also be addressed. Astin (1993) lists the following areas of expertise needed by an assessment expert. These represent the ideal qualifications for an institutional research office committed to the process of a student-centered academic program review. These qualifications combine both technical and political expertise.

Vision: a broad understanding of institutional purposes and ideals

Understanding of academia: a clear conceptual grasp of how academic institutions function

Functional knowledge of measurement and research design: a thorough knowledge of measurement theory, statistical methods, and research design

Technical know-how: familiarity with modern techniques of data collection, data organization, methods of storage and retrieval, and data analysis

Understanding of relevant educational and social science concepts: familiarity with learning theory, instructional methods and theory, curriculum, support services, student development theory, and group dynamics

Good communication skills: ability to listen, speak, and write clearly

Academic qualifications: training, experience, and accomplishments at a level commensurate with appointment as a tenure-track faculty member

To these, we would add the following qualitative research skills: goal-setting experience, interviewing skills, survey construction and analysis skills, focus group experience and group interview skills, and participant observation skills.

No one person is likely to have all the qualifications and skills described here. However, we agree with Astin (1993) that one or more people should have most of these to implement what has been outlined in this chapter.

References

Angelo, T. A., and Cross, K. P. *Classroom Assessment Techniques: A Handbook for College Teachers.* (2nd ed.) San Francisco: Jossey-Bass, 1993.

Association of American Colleges. "Integrity in the College Curriculum: A Report to the Academic Community." Washington, D.C.: Association of American Colleges, 1985.

Association of American Colleges. "The Challenge of Connecting Learning." *Liberal Learning and the Arts and Sciences Major,* 1991a, *1,* 1–33.

Association of American Colleges. "Reports from the Fields." *Liberal Learning and the Arts and Sciences Major,* 1991b, *2,* 1–226.

Association of American Colleges. "Program Review and Educational Quality in the Major." Washington, D.C.: Association of American Colleges, 1992, 3.

Astin, A. *Assessing for Excellence: The Philosophy and Practice of Assessment and Evaluation in Higher Education.* New York: Macmillan, 1993.

Barak, R. J. *Program Review in Higher Education: Within and Without.* Boulder, Colo.: National Center for Higher Education Management Systems, 1982.

Black, L. C. "Portfolio Assessment." In T. Banta and Associates (ed.), *Making a Difference: Outcomes of a Decade of Assessment in Higher Education.* San Francisco: Jossey-Bass, 1993.

Conrad, C. F., and Wilson, R. F. *Academic Program Reviews: Institutional Approaches, Expectations, and Controversies.* ASHE-ERIC Higher Education Report no. 5. Washington, D.C.: Association for the Study of Higher Education, 1985.

Fuhrmann, B. S., and Gentemann, K. M. "A Flexible Approach to Statewide Assessment." In T. Banta and Associates (ed.), *Making a Difference: Outcomes of a Decade of Assessment in Higher Education.* San Francisco: Jossey-Bass, 1993.

Jacobi, M., Astin, A., and Ayala, F., Jr. *College Student Outcome Assessment: A Talent Development Perspective.* ASHE-ERIC Higher Education Report no. 7. Washington, D.C.: Association for the Study of Higher Education, 1987.

Millward, R. E. "Assessment Centers." In T. Banta and Associates (ed.), *Making a Difference: Outcomes of a Decade of Assessment in Higher Education.* San Francisco: Jossey-Bass, 1993.

Morgan, D. *Focus Groups as Qualitative Research.* Newbury Park, Calif.: Sage, 1988.

Peterson, G., and Hayward, P. "Model Indicators of Student Learning in Undergraduate Biology." In C. Adelman (ed.), *Signs and Traces: Model Indicators of College Student Learning in the Disciplines.* Washington, D.C.: Superintendent of Documents, U.S. Government Printing Office, 1989.

Pratt, L., Reichard, D., and Rogers, B. "Designing the Assessment Process." In J. Nichols (ed.), *Institutional Effectiveness and Outcomes Assessment Implementation on Campus: A Practitioner's Handbook.* New York: Agathon Press, 1989.

Ratcliff, J. L. "Development of a Cluster-Analytic Model for Identifying Coursework Patterns Associated with General Learned Abilities of College Students." A paper presented at the Annual Meeting of the American Educational Research Association, New Orleans, April 8, 1988.

Study Group on the Conditions of Excellence in American Higher Education. *Involvement in Learning: Realizing the Potential of American Higher Education.* Sponsored by the National Institute of Education, Washington, D.C., October 1984.

Watt, J. H., and others. "Building Assessment Programs in Large Institutions." In T. Banta and Associates (ed.), *Making a Difference: Outcomes of a Decade of Assessment in Higher Education.* San Francisco: Jossey-Bass, 1993.

Wingspread Group on Higher Education. *An American Imperative: Higher Expectations for Higher Education.* Racine, Wis.: The Johnson Foundation, 1993.

KAREN M. GENTEMANN *is director of institutional assessment, George Mason University, Fairfax, Virginia, and president-elect of the Southern Association for Institutional Research.*

JAMES J. FLETCHER *is associate provost and dean for undergraduate studies, George Mason University, Fairfax, Virginia.*

DAVID L. POTTER *is dean of the College of Arts and Sciences and vice president, George Mason University, Fairfax, Virginia.*

*Exploration of the culture and climate experienced by faculty in a
department or unit can be useful to deans and department chairpersons
committed to understanding, supporting, and leading the faculty of
their unit.*

Understanding and Assessing Faculty Cultures and Climates

Ann E. Austin

Faculty are central to the work of a college or university, and the ways they
understand, interpret, and act on events and circumstances have great import
for the quality of an institution of higher education. Understanding the concepts of faculty culture and unit climate as perceived by the faculty is important for deans and department chairpersons striving to lead their units, to make
good decisions, and to support the work of the faculty.

This chapter explains both the conceptual notions of faculty culture and
climate and how institutional researchers, deans, and department chairpersons
can assess and understand faculty culture and climate. The chapter is organized in three parts. First, the concepts of faculty culture and climate are
defined and explored, with attention to the several cultures to which faculty
belong as well as to the difference between culture and climate. Second, the
chapter explains why it is important for administrators to explore the faculty
cultures and climates of departments, schools, and colleges. Third, the chapter describes specific ways in which institutional researchers, deans, and
department chairpersons can assess and understand faculty culture and climate. This section offers specific strategies, and also raises issues and questions
that institutional researchers and administrative leaders should consider as they
seek to understand faculty culture and climate.

Definitions of Faculty Culture and Climate

Administrative leaders who want to understand and use information about faculty culture and unit climate must have working definitions of these concepts.
This section defines the notion of culture as it relates to faculty, and argues that
faculty members actually work within several relevant cultures. Then, I define

the notion of climate, showing that it is somewhat different from culture. Both concepts hold useful implications for deans, department chairs, and institutional researchers.

Faculty Cultures. Discussions of cultures concern how groups of people construct meaning. Kuh and Whitt (1988) have defined culture as "the collective, mutually shaping patterns of norms, values, practices, beliefs, and assumptions that guide the behavior of individuals and groups" (pp. 12–13). They assert that culture can be understood as "an interpretive framework for understanding and appreciating events and actions" (p. 13). Anthropologist Clifford Geertz (1973, p. 5) has explained that members of groups create "webs of significance"; understanding the culture of a group or organization involves exploring the interpretations, assumptions, and values—the "webs of significance"—deeply embedded and shared by the members. These beliefs, assumptions, and values that contribute to a culture tend to be enduring, changing only slowly over considerable time or in response to a major event, challenge, or crisis (Peterson and Spencer, 1990). In sum, culture has been defined briefly and colloquially as "a kind of 'organizational glue'" (Peterson and Spencer, 1990, p. 7) that is reflected in symbols, widely shared stories and myths, behavioral patterns, and shared beliefs (Clark, 1970; Deal and Kennedy, 1982; Peterson and Spencer, 1990; Schein, 1985).

Although many writers discuss organizational culture, a more complete and useful understanding of faculty culture acknowledges the multiple cultures in which faculty work (Austin, 1990, 1992; Bergquist, 1992; Clark, 1984; Light, Marsden, and Corl, 1972). Faculty are influenced by and must make trade-offs among several cultures, or interpretive frameworks, that affect their conceptualization, understanding, and organization of the faculty role, the balance and integration that they construct among their responsibilities, the degree and nature of their interactions with students, their participation in institutional decision making, and other aspects of their work.

These faculty cultures include the culture of the academic profession, the culture of the academy as an organization, the cultures of particular disciplines, the cultures of institutional types, and the culture of the particular department or unit where the faculty member has a position. Deans, department chairpersons, and institutional researchers seeking to support the work of department and college leaders must understand the values of each of these cultures and the ways in which they interact in the lives of any group of faculty members. The tensions and contradictions among these several cultures are some of the most useful aspects of faculty culture for deans, department chairpersons, and institutional researchers to assess as they seek to understand the lives and work of the faculty in their units.

Culture of the Academic Profession. Across diverse universities, colleges, and disciplines, faculty members share a set of overarching values that are embedded in the academic profession (Clark, 1985; Kuh and Whitt, 1988; Rice, 1986). For example, most faculty members subscribe to the belief that the purposes of higher education are, broadly, to discover, produce, and disseminate knowledge, truth, and understanding. Another core value of the profession is a commitment to serving society. Faculty are socialized in their graduate school experiences to value intellectual autonomy and academic freedom as norms that support creativity, inquiry, and excellence. Peer review and tenure practices have developed institutionally as expressions of the values of autonomy and academic freedom. Other core values of the profession include commitment to intellectual honesty and fairness, as well as commitment to the notion of a community of scholars whose collegiality guides their interactions and their involvement in institutional decision making. Additionally, a belief in the predominant role of research and specialization as the hallmarks of professional excellence has emerged over the past several decades. The distinguished sociologist Burton Clark (1985, p. 42) calls these core values of the academic profession a "super ethos," a culture that crosses institutional and disciplinary lines. However, these values are expressed in different ways depending on institutional and disciplinary contexts.

Culture of the Academy as an Organization. As social organizations, universities and colleges are normative institutions, organizations where members are motivated by the sense that they are involved in significant and good work. Although collegiality and autonomy are central cultural norms in the university and college, the organizational culture also has managerial and bureaucratic elements (Etzioni, 1961; Rice, 1986). In some institutions, external pressures over the past fifteen years (such as fiscal constraints, demands for accountability, and public questioning of the quality of the students produced) have tended to strengthen the bureaucratic and managerial aspects of the culture while diminishing and threatening the normative, collegial culture (Austin and Gamson, 1983). Although not every institution is experiencing this kind of shift in the relationship between the normative and bureaucratic elements in the organization, in many colleges and universities this shift has affected the culture of the daily workplace.

Cultures of the Disciplines. For many faculty at research universities, comprehensive institutions, and liberal arts colleges, the discipline is a particularly strong cultural force and often the primary locus of their professional identity. As explained by Clark (1987, p. 7), disciplines are "the primary units of membership and identification within the academic profession." It is important to note, however, that the primary professional identification for community college faculty is more likely to be with their institutions than with their respective disciplines. Furthermore, within a community college, faculty teaching full-time and those within traditional academic fields are more likely to be influenced by disciplinary cultures than those who teach part-time or who work in professional, vocational, or technical areas.

The graduate school experience typically socializes prospective faculty to the norms, values, beliefs, assumptions, and behavior patterns of their particular disciplines, the department structure serves as the organizational home for the disciplinary culture within a college or university, and the scholarly and professional societies nurture, protect, and maintain the strength of the disciplinary cultures. From the time graduate students begin to prepare for the professoriat and throughout the years of many faculty members' careers, the disciplinary culture affects professional identity, what work is done, what and how much is published, interactions with colleagues and students, criteria for success, and many other facets of professional life (Becher, 1984, 1987; Clark, 1984; Kuh and Whitt, 1988).

For example, in the natural and physical sciences, knowledge is cumulative, with faculty seeking to discover, explain, and identify universal truths. Work is often done in teams, publication rates are fast-paced, competition for success at knowledge discovery is high, and scholars tend to maintain extensive networks through conferences, visits, and informal communications. In the humanities, work is conceptualized and conducted quite differently. Scholars are working to develop interpretations and perspectives rather than universals, they tend to work alone, and publications are fewer and produced more slowly. Other disciplinary areas exhibit their own cultural values, norms, and behavioral patterns (Austin, 1990; Becher, 1984, 1987; Clark, 1984; Kuh and Whitt, 1988). Although the disciplinary cultures are very strong, institutional cultures affect their strength and moderate the extent of their impact on faculty members.

Cultures of Institutional Types. Faculty are affected by the general culture of the profession, by the culture of academic organizations as a whole, and by the cultures of the particular disciplines in which they have been trained and work; they also experience the culture of the institutional type in which they work as well as the unique culture of the specific college or university where they hold a position. The employing institution affects the responsibilities, opportunities, and rewards available to the faculty. In particular, the type of institution in which a faculty member is employed affects his or her relationship to the discipline and its culture, how a new faculty member is socialized, what work is viewed as important, and what standards of excellence are used (Austin, 1990, 1992; Ruscio, 1987).

The several institutional types in academe each tend to have distinct cultures (Clark, 1985, 1987). For example, in major universities, the disciplinary culture is dominant, and faculty derive identity from the disciplinary affiliation, emphasize research, express a cosmopolitan orientation, and value their autonomy. Comprehensive institutions tend to be characterized by focus on undergraduate education along with efforts to emulate the major universities. The resulting culture often involves considerable tension for faculty as they try to carry out research with minimal support while simultaneously facing the demands of heavy teaching duties. Emphasis on teaching and student development characterizes most liberal arts colleges. At the more prestigious ones, faculty members maintain research agendas, but the disciplinary connection is typically weaker at the less prestigious colleges. Heavy teaching loads and diverse student bodies characterize many community colleges. However, Kempner's (1990) exploration of faculty culture at a suburban community college is a reminder that not all institutions of a particular type (in this case, community colleges) share identical cultural norms and values. This advice should be applied to the consideration of culture among any group of institutions.

Institutions of similar type often do share some cultural dimensions, but each institution nevertheless has its own unique culture, which depends on its history, location, faculty and students, patterns of administrative leadership and structures of governance, and other factors (Peterson and others, 1986). For example, at institutions with a strong bureaucratic orientation, faculty are likely to be less involved in decision making and the work environment may tend to be more structured. An institution with a more collegial leadership situation may be more decentralized, characterized by more flexible organizational structures and greater individual autonomy (Austin, 1990; Kuh and Whitt, 1988; Ruscio, 1987).

Culture of the Academic Department. Deans and department chairpersons are likely to be especially interested in the particular cultures of their own units, and perhaps in data that allow for comparisons across departments (which institutional researchers may be able to assist in compiling). Like institutions, departments and other units also have unique cultures characterized by norms, values, and behavior patterns. (Sometimes, departmental cultures are called institutional subcultures.) The departmental mission and goals, the leadership style of the dean, department chairperson, or other administrator, the governance structure of the unit, the characteristics of the students and faculty, the physical environment, and the relationship of the department or unit to other units and to the institution as a whole are all part of the culture of a department.

As the locus for the daily work of faculty members, the department or unit is the site of intersection for the other four cultures discussed. The interaction of these multiple faculty cultures sometimes results in conflicts, tensions, accommodations, or trade-offs for faculty (Austin, 1990; Light, Marsden, and Corl, 1972). For example, disciplinary norms that emphasize specialization and commitment to research and publication may conflict with the values of a teaching-oriented college where faculty must teach across several areas and where criteria for success highlight undergraduate teaching and interactions with students. A department in such a teaching-oriented institution whose faculty are heavily socialized to the disciplinary culture would probably exhibit tension, conflict, and incongruence in its unit culture. In another example, a department may provide a group of service courses that benefit the general education or other undergraduate courses of the institution. Participating faculty may feel that they are exemplifying the value of the academic profession that calls for helping students discover knowledge. If simultaneously the institutional culture values and rewards research over teaching, the departmental culture is likely to reflect incongruence over which values are primary (those of the profession as a whole or those of the institution).

When institutional researchers, deans, and department chairpersons decide to explore the cultures of particular units, they may find it fruitful to ask how multiple faculty cultures intersect within a department or unit. Conflicting values from multiple faculty cultures can create tensions that have direct impact on the work and life within the department or unit.

Implications of Recognizing Multiple Faculty Cultures. The purpose of describing the multiple cultures in which faculty work is not to confuse the issue of assessment of faculty culture. Rather, the purpose is to explain that such assessment should focus on several different dimensions of faculty culture. For example, deans and department chairpersons may be interested in how strongly faculty members in their units subscribe to the values and norms of the academic profession as a whole, their preferred view of the appropriate balance between collegial and bureaucratic elements in an academic organization, the strength of their commitment to their particular disciplinary culture and its values and behavioral patterns, or their assessment of cultural elements specific to the particular institutional type. As another option, deans and department chairpersons may want to focus on the particular and unique culture of their immediate unit. However, consideration of the unit culture should be informed by an understanding that the unit culture may reflect tensions or contradictions in the interactions of the other cultures to which the faculty belong.

Climate. The notion of faculty culture, as discussed in the previous section, concerns the beliefs, values, assumptions, and norms that characterize faculty experience. The previous section argued that faculty experience several different cultures, and that a reference to faculty culture must clarify whether the focus is on the culture of the profession broadly, the academic organization generally, the discipline, the employing institution, or a particular department or unit. Also useful to deans, department chairpersons, and institutional researchers, and somewhat different from culture, is the notion of climate, a concept that comes from social and cognitive psychology and organizational behavior. Whereas *culture* pertains to the embedded and stable beliefs, values, and norms of a group, *climate* refers to members' assessment, views, perceptions, and attitudes toward various aspects of organizational life (Peterson and Spencer, 1990, citing Allaire and Firsirotu, 1984).

Studies of climate often focus on perceptions of such areas as institutional goals, governance and decision making processes, patterns of interaction, workplace dynamics, and faculty morale and satisfaction. With its emphasis on current perceptions and attitudes, climate is more changeable than culture (Peterson and Spencer, 1990). According to Peterson and Spencer (1990, p. 8), "if culture is the 'organizational value,' climate is the 'atmosphere,' or 'style.'" They also suggest that "culture is the meteorological zone in which one lives (tropical, temperate, or arctic) and climate is the daily weather patterns" (p. 8). Although researchers often study climate at the institutional level, there is evidence that department-level work groups can vary in climate and that, given faculty members' orientation to their departments, climate is usefully studied at the unit level as well (Moran and Volkwein, 1988). The concepts of culture and climate can be helpful to institutional researchers, deans, and department chairpersons trying to understand, lead, and support faculty.

Rationale for Exploring Faculty Cultures and Unit Climate

Why should institutional researchers, deans, and department chairpersons make the effort to explore and understand the culture and climate of departmental and college units? Bensimon (1990) asserts that a key responsibility for a president (and, one might add, for a dean and department chairperson) is "interpreting or defining reality for organizational participants" (p. 77). In order to fulfill this responsibility, the leader must understand how shared meanings have evolved and what symbols reflect and nurture these meanings. By understanding the organization or unit as a culture, a leader can develop what Bensimon (1990) calls "a more connected 'we' relationship" rather than a "separate 'they' and 'I' relationship" (p. 78).

Exploration of culture or climate helps leaders better understand the faculty with whom they work and helps the faculty better understand each other. Department faculty members derive meaning, purpose, and a sense of identity from the culture of their unit. The process of assessing and exploring aspects of culture and climate can provide opportunities for faculty to discuss their goals and values, the patterns of interaction, the reward structure, or other dimensions of their workplace (Peterson and Spencer, 1990). Also, cultural analysis can reveal contradictions, problems, dysfunctions, and tensions in an environment, thus opening the way for these concerns to be addressed (Fetterman, 1990). Faculty members sometimes feel that they get mixed messages about what is valued in their units or institutions. By exploring the culture and climate, leaders can see what messages faculty perceive and how the faculty interpret these messages, and they can compare these perceptions with what they intend to convey to the faculty. Culture and climate analysis also can assist administrators to anticipate how faculty members may interpret decisions and actions, and can alert them to when and why resistance may occur. Administrators who understand the culture of their unit will be alert to the symbolic meaning of daily actions and choices (Tierney, 1988).

Cultural awareness on the part of deans and department chairpersons also helps them understand their unit in relation to other units and to the total organization. Tensions and differing viewpoints among different groups within an organization can be more readily understood and addressed when leaders understand the cultural values and assumptions that underlie such dilemmas (Austin, 1990; Kuh, 1990; Tierney, 1988). When deans and department chairpersons understand the deeply held values of the faculty within their units, they can more accurately represent their departments' interests in institutional decision making.

Analysis of unit culture and climate also can be useful in assessing the extent to which a department is actually meeting its goals. For example, Kempner (1990, p. 22) suggests that community college leaders and faculty should ask, "How does our faculty culture facilitate or hinder learning?" A similar question could be equally fruitful for administrators and faculty members in other kinds of colleges and universities to consider. Once leaders and faculty understand how values, assumptions, and behavioral patterns facilitate or hinder the learning process, they can find ways to deal with problems or barriers more effectively.

Another reason for deans and department chairpersons to seek cultural understanding concerns their ability to handle challenges, problems, and crises. In times of crisis, tensions embedded in the culture often become more pronounced. Leaders who understand the culture of their units are better able to consider how to present and handle problems. In fact, they may find ways to use problem definition and solution as opportunities to explore embedded values or to address faculty concerns regarding the unit's climate (Tierney, 1988).

Finally, leaders trying to effect change within their departments and colleges should consider that a unit's cultural values can sometimes preclude faculty from adopting new directions or commitments. Leaders attuned to issues of culture realize that a successful change process requires attention to the implications of the proposed change for the culture and climate of the department or college. If a change process is implemented, measurements of relevant dimensions of the climate over time can be used as benchmarks to monitor the process, impact, and stability of the change (Peterson and Spencer, 1990).

Ways to Assess Faculty Cultures and Unit Climate

The chapter thus far has described the multiple cultures in which faculty live and work and the ways in which those cultures interact within a college, school, or department. Also, it has argued that understanding faculty culture and unit climate should be of importance to deans and department chairpersons and to the institutional researchers interested in supporting such department and college-level activities as planning, decision making, and outcomes assessment. In this section, we discuss practical ways for institutional researchers, deans, and department chairpersons to enhance their understanding of departmental and college culture and climate. First, we explore several issues that should be considered by those seeking to assess culture and climate in a college, school, or department; then, a variety of strategies are described. Throughout the discussion, the intended audience includes institutional researchers, as well as deans and department chairpersons. It is often useful for an administrative leader to call on institutional researchers, who can provide the distance and objectivity of someone not directly involved in the particular unit; however, deans and department chairpersons will find that they can use some of the strategies themselves.

Issues for Consideration When Planning Assessment. Several issues should be considered as institutional researchers or administrative leaders plan to assess unit-level culture or climate.

Purpose and Focus. Institutional researchers, deans, and department chairpersons who want to assess unit-level faculty culture and climate should begin by considering what they want to learn. Do they intend to develop a broad and comprehensive cultural understanding or do they want to understand how faculty perceive certain aspects of the unit's climate? Studies of culture tend to be broad and comprehensive, whereas explorations of climate tend to be more focused and specific, pertaining to faculty members' perceptions (Peterson and Spencer, 1990).

The questions that guide studies of culture versus studies of climate vary somewhat. Leaders interested in assessing the culture of their unit will be interested in the values and assumptions that the faculty hold, the meanings and understandings they gain from situations, policies, and practices, and how those interpretations and meanings influence and guide their behavior. A dean or department chairperson may wonder whether there is congruence among the values held by members of the unit, or whether some of the values and assumptions simultaneously held conflict in their implications.

Another question motivating a study of culture might be the degree of consensus among faculty members in the unit regarding expectations and norms for faculty work. For example, is there consensus or disagreement concerning the extent to which teaching should be valued and rewarded as compared with research activity? Is there a shared sense of what responsibilities the faculty have to the students? Are there subgroups within the faculty and, if so, how do they interpret the unit and its work? Institutional researchers or deans may want to initiate a study that analyzes and compares departmental cultures across a college, school, or university. Information about departmental differences in understanding and valuing faculty outreach and service activities, for example, could be useful as a dean or institutional leader considers tenure or promotion decisions.

If the interest is to assess the unit's climate, a dean or department chairperson, perhaps in consultation with an institutional researcher, should identify the aspects of the climate that are of interest. For example, an assessment of climate might focus on unit goals, decision-making processes, reward structure, workload allocations, faculty evaluation processes, or faculty professional growth opportunities.

Additionally, it is useful to consider the distinctions between the "objective climate," the "perceived climate," and the "psychological or felt climate" (Peterson and Spencer, 1990). The objective climate consists of the patterns of behavior that can be seen by an observer. These might include patterns of faculty and administrator communication, decision-making processes, and forms of faculty–student interaction. However, assessments of climate often also probe the "perceived climate" and the "psychological or felt climate." As

Peterson and Spencer (1990, p. 12) explain, "research on perceived climate focuses on how participants view various institutional patterns and behaviors." For example, studies of perceived climate might focus on faculty members' perceptions of such dimensions of organizational life as unit or institutional goals, decision-making processes, and interpersonal relationships within the workplace. Assessments of the perceived or felt climate explore how members feel about their work and the unit, and often concern faculty members' morale, satisfaction, and commitment to the unit.

As with studies of culture, a central question motivating institutional researchers, deans, and department chairpersons to assess dimensions of the unit's climate might be to determine whether there is consensus among the faculty in their perceptions of the workplace. That is, do the faculty share similar perceptions or attitudes about how decision making occurs or about the equity of the evaluation process and reward structure? Lack of consensus about various aspects of the climate or conflicting perceptions can alert deans and department chairpersons to issues that may need attention. Specific problems or issues may motivate these studies also. For example, a department chairperson's concern about faculty stress might result in an institutional researcher's exploring faculty members' perceptions of the supportiveness of interpersonal relationships as well as the overall levels of faculty commitment, morale, and satisfaction (the "felt" climate).

Methods for Assessment. Those who want to assess culture and climate must consider what methods are most appropriate for their interests and questions. Based on the collection of rich, detailed data, qualitative methods are most useful for exploring cultural issues that concern meaning and significance, such as how faculty make sense of administrative decisions and how faculty perceive the messages embedded in the reward structure. Quantitative methods can provide a sense of the magnitude or extent to which various perceptions are held. For example, survey data provide a validity check for the rich, extensive interpretations that a smaller number of faculty may have shared in individual interviews. Because explorations of culture pertain to questions of interpretation, meaning, and values, qualitative methods (especially interviews and observation) are most useful in studies of culture. Assessments of climate can be served both by quantitative approaches, such as surveys, as well as by qualitative methods, including interviews and participant observation (Marshall, Lincoln, and Austin, 1991; Peterson and Spencer, 1990).

Those who want to understand culture or climate are best served if they use several methods of assessment, triangulating and comparing the findings collected from the various approaches. The use of multiple methods diminishes the limitations inherent in any approach taken alone (Baird, 1990). Using a variety of methods also increases the likelihood that most if not all of the faculty in a department or unit will be involved in some way, and thus can contribute to or influence the conclusions that an institutional researcher, dean, or department chairperson draws. Wide involvement of faculty through the use of a variety of data collection methods (surveys, focus groups, and individual interviews) also enhances the credibility of the process and of the findings (Marshall, Lincoln, and Austin, 1991).

Institutional researchers are likely to be more knowledgeable and experienced than many deans and department chairpersons (whose research specialties may be in areas other than the study of higher education) about a variety of appropriate research methods and about how to make the most productive use of multiple methods of assessing culture and climate. In situations where a dean or department chairperson wishes to design, conduct, or coordinate the strategies for assessing the unit culture or climate, the institutional researcher can advise about methods, assist in data interpretation, and help the unit leader understand findings in the context of the broader institutional culture and climate.

Faculty Concerns. As plans are made to assess a unit's culture and climate, consideration should be given to concerns and questions that may arise among the faculty. If a dean or department chairperson plans to assess the culture and climate more formally and extensively than solely through his or her own listening and observation, it is useful to involve the faculty members in planning the assessment process. Certainly faculty members will want to know why data are being collected and how the data will be used. They also will want to know who will have access to the data, whether their responses to questionnaires will be confidential, and, if interviews are planned, who will be listening to their responses. It is very important for faculty to know that the expression of their views and concerns about the culture or climate will not have a negative impact on them individually or as a unit (Marshall, Lincoln, and Austin, 1991).

The involvement of an institutional researcher can be very helpful as a way to diminish faculty concerns about whether it is safe to express candid viewpoints. An institutional researcher still will be viewed as a representative of the university, however, so he or she also must work to gain credibility and trust. Nevertheless, the institutional researcher may be perceived as a more impartial, less threatening assessor. An institutional researcher (or anyone else conducting such studies) must establish clearly how the confidentiality of the participants will be protected, how the data will be reported, and to whom the data and reports will be provided.

Time and Resources. Decisions about how to assess the culture and climate of a unit must be made with consideration of available time and resources. Deans and department chairpersons, as discussed below, can indeed learn much from their own observation, listening, and exploration of the culture and climate of their units. However, more systematic and extensive assessment efforts require varying amounts of time and effort, depending on the methods used, for institutional researchers, administrative leaders, and the faculty. For example, if a series of interviews is planned, someone must conduct and analyze the data and the faculty must be willing to take the time to participate. Similarly, a survey requires financial resources for design, distribution, and analysis, depending on its extensiveness and the size of the faculty group surveyed.

Time and resource constraints should not deter culture and climate assessment, however. The approaches suggested below can be carried out extensively or more modestly. For example, whereas a department might decide to engage in a year-long series of focus groups or retreats to explore its cultural values and assumptions and their implications for the directions and work of the unit, another department might decide that a short survey focusing on one dimension of the climate (such as the process of annual faculty evaluation) should be the primary concern for that year. Careful assessment of a unit's culture takes time, but a reading of the climate can be done more quickly. Institutional researchers, deans or department chairpersons, and the faculty in their units must consider what methods are appropriate, taking into account the questions or purposes motivating the assessment, the concerns that may arise from the faculty, and the time, resources, and effort that can be directed to the assessment.

Strategies for Assessing Culture and Climate. A variety of strategies, ranging from the casual to the more structured and planned, are available to institutional researchers and administrative leaders seeking to assess cultures and climates within the institution. The first strategy suggested is informal and most useful for deans and department chairpersons themselves to use. The other strategies might be used by an institutional researcher, a dean or a department chairperson, or others invited to assess a unit's culture and climate.

Listening. Even before requesting assistance from institutional researchers, deans and department chairpersons can begin initial assessment of the culture and climate of their unit by being what Bensimon calls a "cultural knower" (1990, p. 83). She explains that a new president "must cultivate and convey the attitude of being a learner and encourage long-time faculty and administrators to explain the institution from their vantage point." The same suggestion can be made to deans and department chairpersons seeking an informal strategy to explore the culture and climate of their units. Good leaders should make it a practice to regularly explore members' shared meanings, but those interested in assessing the culture and climate should be especially attuned to careful listening. This process requires that a leader both listen to the faculty and "engage in sympathetic reflection" (Bensimon, 1990, p. 79, citing Smircich, 1983). The leader can ask himself or herself questions and ponder these questions as the observation and listening proceeds. Bensimon (1990) suggests useful questions that a president might ponder, and variations on these questions would be appropriate for deans and department chairpersons to consider: How do the faculty perceive their role? What beliefs and assumptions do the faculty have about their work, the work of the unit, and how their individual work intersects with the unit work? What symbols, rituals, and routines characterize life in this unit? How are decisions made, who is involved, and who is left out? What issues concern the faculty?

In summary, a dean or department chairperson who wants to understand the culture and climate of the unit should seek opportunities to talk with the faculty, listen deeply, and seek to understand perceptions, interpretations, and meanings from the perspective of the faculty as individuals and as a collective group. This kind of listening requires no funds, but it does demand the commitment and openness of the leader. Furthermore, it takes some time.

Observation. Institutional researchers invited to assist in assessing a college or department's culture or climate, as well as deans and department chairpersons, will find that much can be learned from observation. In particular, institutional leaders and administrative leaders should take note of the behavior patterns of the unit's members over time. How is time spent? What does not get done? Who associates with whom? What are the patterns of interaction? How do faculty interact with students, with support staff, with administrative leaders, and with each other? When and how do faculty express frustration or, conversely, satisfaction? Leaders should also be alert to symbols within the unit, including myths or stories told, traditions observed, celebrations planned, heroes admired, and language used (Deal and Kennedy, 1982). Such symbols and how they are used or recognized reveal a great deal about what a group of people care about. A lack of symbols also indicates something about the culture of a unit; perhaps little attention has been devoted over time to nurturing the expressions of cultural values. The physical environment and arrangements also give hints of the culture of a unit. Is there a common area or are faculty offices spread over a long hall or scattered throughout a building? How do faculty members arrange their offices? Are their doors usually open or routinely closed? Through observation of these kinds of behavior patterns, symbols, and physical arrangements, institutional researchers, deans, and department chairpersons can add significant information to their assessment of unit culture and climate.

Interviews and Other Conversations. One of the most effective qualitative approaches for assessing culture and climate is through interviews and conversations. Institutional researchers, deans, or department chairpersons can schedule interviews with faculty members to provide a vehicle through which the listening process described above can occur more formally. Such interviews can be organized around specific questions about the unit and its culture and climate, or allowed to unfold in a less structured way, guided by a few general questions (such as "what issues are on your mind about the department?" or "tell me about your work"). A variation on individual interviews is the group interview or focused group session. This approach usually works best when one or several aspects of the unit climate are identified as the topic for consideration and when faculty participants are encouraged to brainstorm together about their perceptions of the selected topics. Such group conversations may take place just once or twice, or may be scheduled regularly throughout a semester or academic year. One tool designed to facilitate such conversations is *The Academic Workplace Audit* (Austin, Rice, and Splete, 1991a), which includes sections on organizational culture, faculty and administrative leadership practices, governance structures, faculty development programs, intrinsic and extrinsic rewards, and the nature of colleagueship. Though designed specifically for use in small colleges, many of the questions posed can be adapted to departments or colleges in other institutions.

A variation on periodic group conversations is a retreat at which faculty members and administrators come together for an extended period (perhaps a day or two) to focus their attention together on exploring the culture and climate of their unit. A retreat can be organized around a set of stimulating questions, or might use data from a previously administered survey as a starting point for discussion. Faculty might work as a committee of the whole or in subgroups with time allotted for large-group interaction. In considering any of these forms of conversation, thought should be given to whether the dean or department chairperson will lead the conversation, or whether a faculty member or outside consultant (perhaps an institutional researcher) will facilitate the dialogue. In many departments, conversation is likely to be more open if the unit administrator does not assume the facilitator role. An institutional researcher could be helpful in suggesting consultants with appropriate group facilitation skills, and deans, department chairpersons, and faculty members also often know individuals with knowledge of the particular discipline who might take on the task.

Surveys. Surveys are more useful in exploring perceptions of the unit's climate than in assessing the deeper issues of culture. Surveys can be especially helpful in providing baseline information about aspects of the climate, which can be compared with data collected at a later time, as well as in identifying dimensions of the climate around which faculty hold divergent perceptions. Existing survey instruments and locally designed instruments should be considered. If an existing instrument is selected, it is important to check that the questions asked actually correspond to the issues of interest in the particular unit (Baird, 1990). An instrument designed for and available through the Council of Independent Colleges (Washington, D.C.) called the "Survey of Faculty Views" (Austin, Rice, and Splete, 1991b) includes sections on perceptions of such issues as participation in decision making, evaluation processes, governance issues, and work allocation, as well as measures of faculty morale and satisfaction. Although this survey was designed specifically for use in small colleges and parallels the *Academic Workplace Audit* (Austin, Rice, and Splete, 1991a), it can be adapted to other units. Leaders should recognize, however, that locally designed instruments may be equally or more useful than existing instruments because they can be designed to address specific issues of concern in the unit's climate (Baird, 1990). Involving faculty members in the selection or design of a survey will enhance faculty willingness to respond and interest in the results.

Consultants. A key role for an institutional researcher is to serve as a consultant to colleges and departments interested in assessing culture and climate. As already suggested, it is often wiser for a person external to the unit to conduct interviews, lead retreats, and supervise the collection of survey data, rather than for deans and department chairpersons, or those who report directly to them, to serve in such a role. The involvement of an outsider (such as an institutional researcher) is especially useful if the unit is experiencing tension or if the faculty express distrust of the leader. Also, someone who understands academe but is not part of the unit can sometimes note aspects of the culture or the climate that unit members, due to their daily involvement in the unit, do not readily see. As a consultant, an institutional researcher can become directly involved in carrying out the assessment or can assist a dean, department chairperson, or faculty committee in designing an assessment process and locating an appropriate consultant.

Concluding Thoughts

Efforts to understand the culture and climate experienced by the faculty in their units can provide deans and department chairpersons with very useful perspectives. A variety of strategies can assist leaders who wish to assess culture and climate, and can be used in ways that match the time, resources, and interests of both the leaders and the faculty. With their extensive knowledge of research methods and comprehensive awareness of the institution and its member units, institutional researchers can serve a very important role in helping deans, department chairpersons, and faculty members better understand issues of institutional and unit-level culture and climate. They can remind department chairpersons and deans of the value of studying these issues and can serve as consultants by providing advice or actually carrying out some of the strategies discussed. Additionally, department chairpersons or deans may want institutional researchers to help them develop benchmark measures against which to compare later assessments of culture and climate (Peterson and Spencer, 1990). Finally, an institutional research office can assist deans and department chairpersons to understand their unit-level assessments in the broader context of the institutional culture and climate.

References

Allaire, Y., and Firsirotu, M. E. "Theories of Organizational Culture." *Organizational Studies,* 1984, 5, 193–226.

Austin, A. E. "Faculty Cultures, Faculty Values." In W. G. Tierney (ed.), *Assessing Academic Climates and Cultures.* New Directions for Institutional Research, no. 68. San Francisco: Jossey-Bass, 1990.

Austin, A. E. "Faculty Cultures." In A. I. Morey (ed.), *The Encyclopedia of Higher Education.* Vol. 4. Elmsford, N.Y.: Pergamon Press, 1992.

Austin, A. E., and Gamson, Z. F. *Academic Workplace: New Demands, Heightened Tensions.* ASHE-ERIC Higher Education Report no. 10. Washington, D.C.: Association for the Study of Higher Education, 1983.

Austin, A. E., Rice, R. E., and Splete, A. P. *The Academic Workplace Audit.* Washington, D.C.: The Council of Independent Colleges, 1991a.

Austin, A. E., Rice, R. E., Splete, A. P., and Associates. *A Good Place to Work.* Washington, D.C.: The Council of Independent Colleges, 1991b.

Baird, L. L. "Campus Climate: Using Surveys for Policy-Making and Understanding." In W. G. Tierney (ed.), *Assessing Academic Climates and Cultures.* New Directions for Institutional Research, no. 68. San Francisco: Jossey-Bass, 1990.

Becher, T. "The Cultural View." In B. R. Clark (ed.), *Perspectives on Higher Education: Eight Disciplinary and Comparative Views.* Los Angeles: University of California Press, 1984.

Becher, T. "The Disciplinary Shaping of the Profession." In B. R. Clark (ed.), *The Academic Profession: National, Disciplinary, and Institutional Settings.* Los Angeles: University of California Press, 1987.

Bensimon, E. M. "The New President and Understanding the Campus." In W. G. Tierney (ed.), *Assessing Academic Climates and Cultures.* New Directions for Institutional Research, no. 68. San Francisco: Jossey-Bass, 1990.

Bergquist, W. H. *The Four Cultures of the Academy: Insights and Strategies for Improving Leadership in Collegiate Organizations.* San Francisco: Jossey-Bass, 1992.

Clark, B. R. *The Distinctive College: Antioch, Reed, Swarthmore.* Chicago: Aldine, 1970.

Clark, B. R. *The Higher Education System: Academic Organization in Cross-National Perspective.* Los Angeles: University of California Press, 1984.

Clark, B. R. "Listening to the Professoriate." *Change,* 1985, *17* (5), 36–43.

Clark, B. R. *The Academic Life: Small Worlds, Different Worlds.* Princeton, N.J.: Carnegie Foundation for the Advancement of Teaching, 1987.

Deal, T. E., and Kennedy, A. A. *Corporate Cultures: The Rites and Rituals of Corporate Life.* Reading, Mass.: Addison-Wesley, 1982.

Etzioni, A. *A Comparative Analysis of Complex Organizations: On Power, Involvement, and Their Correlates.* (2nd ed.) New York: Free Press, 1961.

Fetterman, D. M. "Ethnographic Auditing: A New Approach to Evaluating Management." In W. G. Tierney (ed.), *Assessing Academic Climates and Cultures.* New Directions for Institutional Research, no. 68. San Francisco: Jossey-Bass, 1990.

Geertz, C. *The Interpretation of Cultures.* New York: Basic Books, 1973.

Kempner, K. "Faculty Culture in the Community College: Facilitating or Hindering Learning?" *The Review of Higher Education,* 1990, *13* (2), 215–235.

Kuh, G. D. "Assessing Student Culture." In W. G. Tierney (ed.), *Assessing Academic Climates and Cultures.* New Directions for Institutional Research, no. 68. San Francisco: Jossey-Bass, 1990.

Kuh, G. D., and Whitt, E. J. *The Invisible Tapestry: Culture in American Colleges and Universities.* ASHE-ERIC Higher Education Report no. 1. Washington, D.C.: Association for the Study of Higher Education, 1988.

Light, D. W., Jr., Marsden, L. R., and Corl, T. C. *The Impact of the Academic Revolution on Faculty Careers.* AAHE-ERIC Higher Education Research Report no. 10. Washington, D.C.: American Association of Higher Education, 1972.

Marshall, C., Lincoln, Y. S., and Austin, A. E. "Integrating a Qualitative and Quantitative Assessment of the Quality of Academic Life: Political and Logistical Issues." In D. M. Fetterman (ed.), *Using Qualitative Methods in Institutional Research.* New Directions for Institutional Research, no. 72. San Francisco: Jossey-Bass, 1991.

Moran, E. T., and Volkwein, J. F. "Examining Organizational Climate in Institutions of Higher Education." *Review of Higher Education,* 1988, *28* (4), 367–383.

Peterson, M. W., and others. *The Organizational Context for Teaching and Learning: A Review of the Research Literature.* Ann Arbor: National Center for Research to Improve Postsecondary Teaching and Learning, University of Michigan, 1986.

Peterson, M. W., and Spencer, M. G. "Understanding Academic Culture and Climate." In W. G. Tierney (ed.), *Assessing Academic Climates and Cultures.* New Directions for Institutional Research, no. 68. San Francisco: Jossey-Bass, 1990.

Rice, R. E. "The Academic Profession in Transition: Toward a New Social Fiction." *Teaching Sociology,* 1986, *14,* 12–23.

Ruscio, K. P. "Many Sectors, Many Professions." In B. R. Clark (ed.), *The Academic Profession: National, Disciplinary, and Institutional Settings.* Los Angeles: University of California Press, 1987.

Schein, E. H. *Organizational Culture and Leadership: A Dynamic View.* San Francisco: Jossey-Bass, 1985.

Smircich, L. "Concepts of Culture and Organizational Analysis." *Administrative Science Quarterly,* 1983, *28,* 339–358.

Tierney, W. G. "Organizational Culture in Higher Education." *Journal of Higher Education,* 1988, *59,* 2–21.

ANN E. AUSTIN is associate professor in the Higher, Adult, and Lifelong Education Program at Michigan State University.

One major way to respond to internal and external pressure for change in the current faculty culture is with a redefinition of faculty work.

Defining Faculty Work

Peter J. Gray, Robert M. Diamond

This is the first of two chapters that focus on defining, assigning, and assessing faculty work. In this chapter, a planned change process is proposed and described as the vehicle for redefining faculty work. Then *legitimate faculty work* is defined in broad terms. Next, we identify and describe multiple information sources and methods for collecting information that support this redefining process. The final step in redefining faculty work is the development of new mission statements for the institution and its academic units. In Chapter Six, we describe a process for assigning and assessing faculty work and the roles for institutional researchers, deans, and department chairs.

As earlier chapters in this volume have discussed, higher education is being pressured to change in fundamental ways. Legislatures, boards of trustees, parents, the media, various academic disciplines and professional associations, and accrediting organizations are calling on higher education to demonstrate greater responsiveness to an increasingly diverse student body and to the increasingly acute problems of society. At the same time, demands are being made that higher education become more efficient and effective in its use of dwindling resources. Higher education faculty, in particular, are seen by many as unresponsive, narrowly focused, and inefficient, especially when it comes to their teaching.

In many cases, these perceptions of faculty are simply not true. As Kerr states (1994, p. 12), "In the main, I have been much impressed by the quality and fairness of teaching, even though it is not subject to much external scrutiny and usually is not rewarded adequately even when of the highest quality. It is as good as it is mostly because academics are interested in their subjects, do not like to fail in any endeavor they undertake, and have a well-developed 'instinct of workmanship.' "

Faculty culture like any other culture, is resistant to change. The processes that have evolved in the United States to educate, select, reward, and protect faculty to be productive and creative scholars now act as forces to limit the

NEW DIRECTIONS FOR INSTITUTIONAL RESEARCH, no. 84, Winter 1994 © Jossey-Bass Publishers

impact society can have on changing faculty culture. Furthermore, demographic and economic conditions over the last ten to fifteen years have led to large numbers of faculty being tenured, thereby enhancing their autonomy. Together, these processes and conditions inhibit the opportunity to change what faculty prefer or have been prepared to do and what they are expected to do. The conservative nature of faculty culture also is evident in its resistance to changes in the processes used to document what faculty actually do in their professional work and to evaluate how well they do it.

Of course, these concerns are manifested to different degrees in various institutions depending on their traditions and culture, especially regarding faculty autonomy. For example, in community colleges and many small four-year liberal arts and comprehensive colleges, there is fairly strong agreement on the primary role of the faculty member as teacher. Even in these institutions, however, faculty may have considerable control over defining faculty work to fit with their interests and specializations. There also may be a discrepancy between the rhetoric regarding the importance of teaching and the reality of the importance of research in hiring and rewarding faculty in these institutions, a situation often found in doctorate-granting and research universities. In addition, in doctorate-granting and research universities there is typically less control by administrators and even more autonomy, especially among senior, tenured faculty, over how faculty spend their time and how they are evaluated and rewarded.

In all institutions, to achieve a reasonable balance of interests, administrators of academic units must mediate between the pressures for change and their faculty colleagues' natural resistance to change. The focus of this chapter is at the unit level, where faculty culture is strongest. This is typically the level where faculty members' affiliation to their academic discipline also is manifested. Depending on the size of the institution, this mediation and affiliation takes place in what is called a division, school, college, department, or program.

A more concrete way to define the unit level is to determine the point where faculty rewards and support are most directly controlled or allocated, that is, where annual salary increases are determined; initial promotion and tenure decisions are made; graduate assistant assignments (research and teaching) are allocated; sabbatical leaves are granted; computer equipment, telephones, and clerical or office staff assistance are made available; and travel funds are provided. At this level, the influence of the local faculty culture is most focused. This structure has both positive and negative implications. It means that the potential for influencing change is the greatest where the resources are controlled, but it also means that the present cultural norms are also the strongest. Administrators at the unit level, such as deans, department chairs, program directors, and unit administrators, must act as the direct mediators between the present cultural norms and the redefined role of faculty, using the means most likely to influence change.

Accomplishing Planned Changes

Institutional researchers can play an active role in campuswide change efforts and can support change at the unit level. The most efficient and effective use of the limited human and financial resources available in most institutional research offices is to begin by working with upper-level administrators to develop the institutional context for change. Then, together with upper-level administrators, institutional researchers can identify those academic units with administrators and faculty who are sympathetic to the need for change in the campus culture and who have a track record of success. These units are often early and successful adopters of innovation and are often perceived as opinion leaders among their administrative and faculty colleagues. As a result, they can act as role models for change.

Planned Change. We propose the use of a planned change process to redefine, assign, and assess faculty work. Planned change processes, designed to describe current conditions and set future directions, emphasize the importance of involvement of those most likely to be affected by the change. This involvement is especially important in the collegial culture of higher education. "The colleges and universities that do well and improve themselves at a time of contradiction and retrenchment are those where the faculty is invited to participate in hard decisions rather than being told what those decisions are" ("Education Life," 1994, p. 18).

The task of defining faculty work anew is the initial stage in a planned change process aimed at modifying the culture of higher education to recognize and reward a broader range of faculty work. The result of this stage is the development of an ideal comprehensive definition of faculty work. The second stage, assigning faculty work, involves the development of realistic interpretations of faculty work as administrators and faculty negotiate the actual assignment of faculty work.

The third stage, assessing faculty work, focuses on operationalizing the first two stages through the documentation and judgment of the quality of the work performed. To complete the planned change process, information gathered in the final stage is fed back into the system. This feedback can be used to make decisions about the accomplishments of individual faculty and about future changes needed in the culture of unit, particularly the ways in which the unit defines its work, negotiates the assignment of work, and assesses this work.

Given the limited resources of their offices, institutional researchers' primary effort should be to work with a campus leadership team to develop models that can be adopted and adapted by individual units. Working with upper-level administrators and a small group of key unit administrators and faculty, institutional researchers can help develop model procedures for defining, assigning, and assessing faculty work within an institution. These model procedures can then be adopted and adapted for use by other units.

In planning for the dissemination of such models, the following stages of planned change should be taken into consideration (Owens, 1970, p. 148):

Awareness: when people first realize that there is a need to change and that some innovation for facilitating this change does exist.

Personal interest: when people begin to understand the impact the change is likely to have on them individually and collectively.

Evaluation: when people think through an idea to determine how it might work in their particular situation.

Trial: when people engage in a small-scale application of the idea to test its applicability and feasibility.

Adoption/adaptation: when people decide to adopt the innovation by adapting it to their local conditions.

Many institutional researchers have been involved in planned change processes, such as strategic planning, total quality management, organizational development, and continuous quality improvement. Based on these experiences, they can provide assistance in the development of strategies and timelines that are sensitive to the stages people and units go through and ones that can lead to the adoption of the models created by a team of upper-level administrators and key unit administrators and faculty members.

Leadership. What is needed most for planned change to be successful is leadership and support from administrators at higher levels, such as deans of large schools or colleges, as well as from provosts, vice presidents for academic affairs, presidents, or chancellors. These upper-level administrators must not only set the direction for change through their words, but ultimately they must act to provide the new resources or to reallocate existing resources, which will be used by unit-level administrators as rewards and support to bring about changes in the local unit culture.

Institutional researchers and the leadership team must be aware of the political nature of change in higher education within which faculty work at the unit level is defined. In this regard, implementing new definitions of faculty work that are consistent with the changing realities of higher education will take considerable leadership ability at the institutional and unit levels.

The unique culture of the academy requires a special approach to leadership. That is, "in professional organizations, leaders might not directly control professionals. Mobilizing resources in such organizations takes place within a network of complex relationships referred to as 'collegiality' " (Curry, 1992, p. 21). Because of the collegial nature of the academy, Curry (p. 22) suggests that faculty and administrators usually "do not expect change to come as dicta from inaccessible individuals." Instead, "When members of an organization enjoy a fair amount of autonomy, such as that enjoyed by faculty, decisions related to implementing and institutionalizing innovations cannot be made unilaterally and be expected to go uncontested" (Curry, 1992, p. 22). Therefore, it is to be expected that the mere idea, as well as the substance, of changes in the definition of faculty work will be the focus of intense debate and discussion, especially at the unit level. This is as much a result of faculty members' natural resistance to change as of their natural tendency to question authority. The role of the administrator is to facilitate change while maintaining collegial relationships.

Challenge of Change. Because the local faculty culture is focused most strongly within academic units (whether they are called schools, colleges, divisions, departments, or programs), deans, chairs, and directors are the ones who must offer the invitation to faculty "to participate in hard decisions" related to changing the local culture" ("Education Life," 1994, p. 18). Upper-level administrators, however, must set the example by inviting key administrators and faculty members to become involved in the development of new institutional teams for defining, assigning, and assessing faculty work. Institutional researchers can facilitate this process by providing such a team with the information and methods necessary to deal with the political, personal, and interpersonal issues that must be addressed if a new concept of faculty work is going to be developed to take American higher education institutions into the twenty-first century.

As the *Times* article warns ("Education Life," 1994, p. 16), "The question is no longer whether to retract, consolidate, restructure, and adapt in order to bear down on the basic mission of higher education—preparing students to take part in their civilization—but whether these reforms can be accomplished from within or must be imposed from without. The answer will be determined in large part by the outcome of a struggle—some call it a shoot out—now in progress around the country between administrators and faculties."

In summary, in order to accomplish fundamental changes in the culture of higher education, the process of defining, assigning, and assessing faculty members' work must be dramatically altered. To successfully alter this process, administrators and faculty members must have leadership from those at upper levels of the campus administration. They must also have access to information and methods that institutional researchers can best provide. The purpose of the following discussion is to describe the role of the institutional researcher in working with a team of upper-level administrators, unit-level administrators, and faculty members to develop new models for defining faculty work.

Defining Faculty Work

The way faculty work is defined has become considerably more complex since the time in 1869 when Charles W. Eliot, then president of Harvard University said, "the prime business of American professors . . . must be regular and assiduous class teaching" (cited in Boyer, 1990, p. 4). In the last 125 years, the definition of faculty work has changed to include a major emphasis on research. As a result, today "the research mission, which was appropriate for some institutions, [has] created a shadow over the entire higher learning enterprise" (Boyer, 1990, pp. 12–13). These changes in definition have inevitably caused tension among different generations of faculty members within institutions. As numerous national reports, scholarly studies, and articles in the popular media indicate, there are tensions between those responsible for higher education (administrators and faculty members) and undergraduate students, their parents, and others, who all define the job of the professor quite differently. These differing perspectives are especially apparent regarding the relative importance of the various aspects of faculty work.

The feeling is slowly developing in the higher education community that faculty work must be redefined in terms of a broader variety of activities than has been the norm and that the faculty reward system must be sensitive to the amount and quality of faculty time and effort expended in relation to this broader variety of activities (Diamond and Adam, 1993). This redefinition can lead to a better balance of faculty effort if it results in faculty members devoting a reasonable amount of time and effort to all of the tasks needed to accomplish the mission of their units and institutions.

Toward a Broader Definition of Faculty Work. As a result of recent close scrutiny, the complexity of faculty members' work has become apparent. Braskamp and Ory's *Assessing Faculty Work* (1994) contains an excellent discussion on classifying faculty work, as do the publications they cite (Bowen and Schuster, 1986; Boyer, 1990; Rhodes, 1990; Rice, 1991). In addition, Ernest Boyer's keynote speech at the January 1994 American Association for Higher Education's Faculty Roles and Rewards Conference provided a comprehensive description of faculty work. The recent monograph *Recognizing Faculty Work: Reward Systems for the Year 2000* (Diamond and Adam, 1993) includes a discussion of changing roles and the faculty reward system (Diamond, 1993) and a description of differences among the disciplines regarding an expanded definition of faculty work (Adam and Roberts, 1993).

Clearly, the current movement is about more than simply restoring a balance among the faculty roles of teaching, service, and research. It really concerns a recognition of the complexity of what professors do. In this regard, legitimate faculty work may be defined to include the following:

Working with students in many different settings and using many different methods for teaching undergraduates and graduates; advising prospective students to postdoctoral fellows; and interacting informally out of class

Professional citizenship involving serving on departmental, school, or institutional committees; assuming leadership roles within the institution and in professional organizations; and representing the institution on external committees, task forces, commissions, and other agencies

Scholarly activity involving research that leads to the production of intellectual or creative works and writing for publication, presentation, or performance

Professional service through editing of professional publications and the application of disciplinary expertise to assist local, regional, national, and international institutions (including one's own college or university), communities, citizen groups, government agencies, businesses, and industry

The process of defining, assigning, assessing, and eventually rewarding faculty work must take this complexity into account.

Information and Methods for Defining Faculty Work. There are several sources of information and methods for gathering information that can facilitate the development of new definitions of faculty work. For example, one activity that can help to define faculty work is the analysis of past and current documentation describing faculty roles, which can be found in externally and internally produced documents and data bases. By comparing and contrasting how the contents of such documents and data bases have changed, it is possible to understand how current ideas about faculty work were formed. This understanding provides the foundation for the redefinition of faculty work.

External Documents and Data Bases. Institutional researchers can work with a campus leadership team to identify relevant historical documents and data bases external to an institution. Such documents might include the following:

Reports such as the UCLA Higher Education Research Institute study on the American college teacher (Astin, Korn, and Dey, 1991), *Teaching, Research, and Faculty Rewards* (Fairweather, 1993), and *Faculty Workload: Research, Theory, and Interpretation* (Yuker, 1984)

Information from studies conducted by the National Center for Education Statistics, the Education Commission of the States, the National Center for Higher Education Management Systems, and the members of the Higher Education Data Sharing Consortium

State mandates, charters, or legislation regarding legitimate faculty roles and their relative importance in relation to particular types of institutions or units

Statements by academic disciplines and professional associations that describe legitimate faculty roles for their members (see the statements in Adam and Roberts, 1993, and others available in Diamond and Adam, in press)

Accreditation guidelines, regulations, and standards for institutions and academic units

Examples of mission statements, promotion and tenure guidelines, and similar documents from comparable institutions

The Pister report (Pister, 1991), written for the University of California, Berkeley, is a good example of an effort to identify relevant documents and statements that have influenced the definition of faculty work over time.

Internal Documents and Data Bases. By working with the campus leadership team, institutional researchers also can identify prototype documents and data bases within an institution. In fact, institutional research offices may be responsible for developing documents or for maintaining relevant data bases such as the following:

Institutional: mission statements; strategic plans; major policy speeches and other relevant public documents from presidents and upper-level administrators; affirmative action plans; faculty contracts; faculty workload policies; faculty and student recruitment materials; faculty handbooks; senate committee documents on teaching, research, and service; hiring, promotion, merit pay, and tenure guidelines; faculty sabbatical leave guidelines; and teaching and research award guidelines

Faculty: course load; course-level responsibility; faculty–student ratios; average contact hours; distribution of faculty advising and other out-of-class responsibilities by student level; the relation of teaching and research responsibilities to faculty rank changes and salary increments (reported in the local American Association of University Professors, Annual Committee Z report); and other factors related to equity of work load, pay, promotion, and tenure

Students: patterns of course enrollment and enrollment by majors or programs; student satisfaction and involvement in activities for which faculty are responsible; student learning, retention, and graduation; and alumni success and satisfaction

Unit-level versions of this institutional information also may be available. In addition, there may be unique information available at the unit level that suggests the past and present official definition of faculty work, such as charters or descriptions, self-study documents created as part of accreditation reviews, and specific handbooks and guides for advising or other faculty activities.

Having once identified relevant documents and data bases a team of upper-level administrators and key unit administrators and faculty can compile a rich library of information for use by others at the unit level. This information can be especially useful in clarifying issues related to the equitable distribution and reward of faculty work and how these issues have changed over time.

The historical picture of changes in the definition of faculty work and the resulting distribution of work loads and rewards will show clearly the relative value that has been placed on various types of faculty work. By considering this information in their efforts to redefine faculty work, administrators and faculty members can create definitions and reward systems that are appropriate for current conditions.

Institutional researchers can help the leadership team to identify institutional and unit-level sources of information regarding the definition of faculty work and how it has changed over time. They can also suggest methods for collecting, analyzing, synthesizing, summarizing, and using this information to provide a picture of the official definition of faculty work relevant to a local academic culture. This information is contextualized through the personal perspectives described next.

Personal Perspectives. There also are various unofficial sources of information available about the campus culture (the way things were, the way they are, and the way they should be in the future). These include the collective history and perceptions of the people who make up an institution and its units: its schools, colleges, divisions, departments, and programs. Although these sources of information are largely personal and, in some cases, may provide data that are quite anecdotal, they are no less relevant to the redefinition of faculty work than factual information from official sources. The purpose of gathering personal information is to lend a human face to the official definition of faculty work.

People in each discipline, at every stage of their career, and with all varieties of responsibilities, interests, and talents will have very different views about what it means to be a faculty member. Taken together, these views form the culture of an institution and its units. The perspectives of faculty members in the following categories should be sought in order to ensure that a broad spectrum of personal points of view are understood: those who represent the full range of positions in the institution; those who came to the institution during different eras in its history; those who are in different stages of their careers; those who are located in a cross-section of academic disciplines, departments, and programs; and those who represent a diversity of religious, political, racial, ethnic, and other groups.

Students (undergraduate and graduate, full-time and part-time, traditional-aged and older) will also have very different points of view about what it means to be a faculty member, as will staff members and administrators. The same is true for off-campus constituents such as alumni, employers, parents, community leaders, and citizens. These points of view should be explicated and included in the conversation about the definition of faculty work when appropriate and feasible.

The standard methods used by institutional researchers to collect, organize, analyze, and summarize qualitative information are appropriate here. For example, focus groups, face-to-face and telephone interviews, and surveys of a sample of people across an institution are efficient ways to gather personal perspectives. Institutional researchers can help the leadership team develop a true picture of the campus culture by suggesting appropriate methods for identifying the strongest candidates, for organizing and conducting the collection of information, and for summarizing and reporting results. Qualitative information collected from on-campus sources may be guided by questions such as the following: What did faculty work mean to you at the beginning of your career or when you first became associated with this institution? What does it mean to you now? How do you think it will change in the future? What are the influences that have caused you to change your view of faculty work? How do you think your definition of faculty work is similar to or different from that of others at this institution? What do you think are the reasons behind these similarities and differences?

Syracuse Survey. A method that institutional researchers might suggest as a model to collect information about the campus culture and faculty members' perceptions is a survey developed at Syracuse University. This survey measures the perceptions of faculty, department chairs, deans, and central administrators regarding the relative importance of research and undergraduate teaching (Gray, Froh, and Diamond, 1992). Survey items focus on people's own opinions and their perceptions of others on campus regarding these two important faculty roles. In addition, respondents are asked to indicate the direction in which their institution is going and the direction in which it should go concerning the relative importance of undergraduate teaching and research. An open-ended item asks respondents to discuss the reasons behind their responses.

The Syracuse University survey was first administered to nearly 50,000 people from forty-seven research and doctorate-granting institutions, resulting in more than 23,000 respondents (Gray, Froh, and Diamond, 1992). Currently, this survey is being administered at 200 other institutions, including more than 150 comprehensive and four-year liberal arts colleges. The second phase of the study is expected to result in more than 30,000 additional respondents (Adam, Diamond, Froh, and Gray, 1994).

The information gathered by the survey has helped the campuses involved to focus attention on the range and balance of faculty work at the institutional and unit level. Following the survey, there have often been campuswide meetings of upper-level administrators, unit administrators, and faculty to discuss the survey results. These meetings have led to the development of unit plans for changing the definition of faculty work and the reward system on campuses across the country (Roberts, Wergin, and Adam, 1993). Available from the Syracuse University Center for Instructional Development, this survey can be adapted for local use to help reveal consistencies and inconsistencies in the intrinsic and extrinsic value placed on different kinds of work by administrators and faculty members within units and across campus.

AACSB Survey. Another method of gathering information about the definition of faculty work is a survey developed at Syracuse University for the American Assembly of Collegiate Schools of Business (AACSB). This survey consists of statements defining faculty work, in terms of a very broad range of activities and products, that were developed by the AACSB task force (Laidlaw, 1992). The survey presents statements about various products and activities grouped under three categories: basic scholarship, applied knowledge, and instructional development. Respondents are asked to indicate the value they place on these products and activities and the value they believe that their unit's reward systems place on the products or activities.

Responses by more than 3,000 faculty members in approximately 175 institutions resulted in several interesting findings. For all but two items, faculty members valued the entire range of products and activities more highly than they were perceived to be valued by the unit's reward systems. The two instances in which the value in the unit's reward system was perceived as higher than faculty members' personal value were related to publications in refereed journals. The greatest discrepancies between the value that faculty place on activities and products and the value they ascribe to their unit's reward system were related to the applied scholarship category, in activities such as "interpreting real world experiences to classroom use that is generalized and reusable" and "interdisciplinary work across fields" (Diamond, Gray, and Wasserman, 1994).

Surveys such as those just described can be used to explicate the differences between personal perceptions and the points of view presented in official documents and formal reward systems. In addition, they can highlight differences in perceptions among the various groups on campus, such as those in different positions (faculty and administrators), those in different disciplines, and those at different stages of their careers.

In Summary. Information gathered by the review of official documents and data bases as well as that collected using qualitative and survey methods can provide a basis for discussions regarding the redefinition of faculty work at the unit level. The results can provide a reality check for the official rhetoric embodied in formal documents. It is often enlightening to the authors of official documents and to those affected by them to see the consistencies and inconsistencies that exist among these definitions and between official definitions and individuals' definitions.

Institutional researchers can offer the greatest service by providing the tools a campus team of upper-level administrators and key unit administrators and faculty members can use to gather information and then compare and contrast the pictures presented by the document and data base analyses with the personal histories and perceptions.

Valuable resources in providing these tools include publications in the Association for Institutional Research's Resources for Institutional Research series, such as *Reference Sources: An Annotated Bibliography for Institutional Research* (Fendley and Seeloff, 1993) and *Questionnaire Survey Research: What Works* (Suskie, 1992). In addition, the Sage Publications Applied Social Research Methods Series has a number of relevant volumes, such as those on *Survey Research Methods* (Fowler, 1984), *Secondary Research: Information Sources and Methods* (Stewart, 1984), *Case Study Research: Design and Methods* (Yin, 1984), and *Diagnosing Organizations: Methods, Models, and Processes* (Harrison, 1987).

Mission Statements

Using the information gathered from official sources and personal perceptions, model mission statements can be developed. Mission statements are often perceived as vague platitudes chiseled over the entrance to a school or articulated at the beginning of recruitment and printed in public relations materials. However, institutions and the units within them also have specific missions, whether they are explicitly or implicitly stated.

Of course, many differences exist among institutions of various sizes and identities, such as community colleges, four-year comprehensive and liberal arts colleges, and research universities, as well as among units within these institutions. A major challenge for institutional researchers is to help the leadership team focus on the most relevant information and develop models that reflect a synthesis of all the quantitative and qualitative information gathered about an institution and its units into succinct and meaningful mission statements.

Mission statements should have three elements. The first element, the purpose, should combine societal and institutional needs and faculty strengths and interests as they are related to the institution or unit's unique reason for being. This statement can also serve as a rationale by explaining the reasons behind the unique mission of the institution or unit.

The second element is a general description of the range of potential responsibilities of faculty members in relation to the purpose or rationale of the institution or unit. That is, how faculty are expected to work with students, assume professional citizenship, engage in scholarly activity, and perform professional service should be described in ways that are germane to the institution's or unit's reason for being.

Closely related to the general description of the range of potential responsibilities of faculty members is the third element of the mission statement, which indicates the relative importance of various faculty functions, roles, and activities. Some activities may be more or less important in particular institutions, their relative emphasis or importance among the units in an institution may vary, and their importance to individual faculty may be different at various times. It is essential for mission statements to recognize these differences because they influence the assignment, the assessment, and, ultimately, the rewarding of faculty work. Through internal and external documents and data bases, as well as the perceptions of key people at the institution, an appropriate set of functions, roles, and activities can be developed that represent the range of faculty work and the variety and level of effort that is necessary for institutions and individual units to accomplish their missions.

Of course, mission statements vary widely, and each one is unique in many ways depending on the type and size of the institution or unit, its history, and its current role in the higher education community. As model strategies of planned change are developed to assist institutions and units in their redefinition of faculty work, institutional researchers must keep in mind these variations and other important factors related to the culture of higher education, such as the collegial nature of the campus community and the critical role that faculty across campus must play in order to ensure the success of any change effort. These considerations lead to Chapter Six and the next topic, the assignment and assessment of faculty work.

References

Adam, B. E., Diamond, R. M., Froh, R. C., and Gray, P. J. *A National Study on the Balance Between Research and Undergraduate Teaching—Phase II: A Report to Participating Institutions.* Syracuse, N.Y.: Syracuse University Center for Instructional Development, 1994.

Adam, B. E., and Roberts, A. O. "Differences Among the Disciplines." In R. M. Diamond and B. E. Adam (eds.), *Recognizing Faculty Work: Reward Systems for the Year 2000.* New Directions for Higher Education, no. 81. San Francisco: Jossey-Bass, 1993.

Astin, A. W., Korn, W. S., and Dey, E. L. *The American College Teacher: National Norms for the 1989–1990 HERI Faculty Survey.* Los Angeles: Higher Education Research Institute, UCLA Graduate School of Education, 1991.

Bowen, H. R., and Schuster, J. H. *American Professors: A National Resource Imperiled.* New York: Oxford University Press, 1986.

Boyer, E. L. *Scholarship Reconsidered: Priorities for the Professoriate.* Princeton, N.J.: Carnegie Foundation for the Advancement of Teaching, 1990.

Braskamp, L. A., and Ory, J. C. *Assessing Faculty Work: Enhancing Individual and Institutional Performance.* San Francisco: Jossey-Bass, 1994.

Curry, B. K. *Instituting Enduring Innovations: Achieving Continuity of Change in Higher Education.* ASHE-ERIC Higher Education Report no. 7. Washington, D.C.: The George Washington University School of Education and Human Development, 1992.

Diamond, R. M. "Instituting Change in the Faculty Reward System." In R. M. Diamond and B. E. Adam (eds.), *Recognizing Faculty Work: Reward Systems for the Year 2000.* New Directions for Higher Education, no. 81. San Francisco: Jossey-Bass, 1993.

Diamond, R. M., and Adam, B. E. (eds.). *Recognizing Faculty Work: Reward Systems for the Year 2000.* New Directions for Higher Education, no. 81. San Francisco: Jossey-Bass, 1993.

Diamond, R. M., and Adam, B. E. (eds.). *Statements from the Disciplines: The Work of Faculty.* Washington, D.C.: American Association for Higher Education, in press.

Diamond, R. M., Gray, P. J., and Wasserman, T. H. *American Assembly of Collegiate Schools of Business: Faculty Survey on the Value of Various Forms of Faculty Work.* Syracuse, N.Y.: Syracuse University Center for Instructional Development, 1994.

"Education Life." *New York Times,* January 9, 1994, pp. 16–18.

Fairweather, J. S. (coord.). *Teaching, Research, and Faculty Rewards: A Summary of the Research Findings of the Faculty Profile Project.* University Park, Pa.: National Center on Postsecondary Teaching, Learning, and Assessment, 1993.

Fendley, W. R., and Seeloff, L. T. (eds.). *Reference Sources: An Annotated Bibliography for Institutional Research.* Resources for Institutional Research, no. 8. Tallahassee, Fla.: Association for Institutional Research, 1993.

Fowler, F. J., Jr. *Survey Research Methods.* Applied Social Research Methods Series, vol. 1. Newbury Park, Calif.: Sage, 1984.

Gray, P. J., Froh, R. C., and Diamond, R. M. *A National Study of Research Universities on the Balance Between Research and Undergraduate Teaching.* Syracuse, N.Y.: Syracuse University, Center for Instructional Development, 1992.

Harrison, M. I. *Diagnosing Organizations: Methods, Models, and Processes.* Applied Social Research Methods Series, vol. 8. Newbury Park, Calif.: Sage, 1987.

Kerr, C. "Knowledge Ethics and the New Academic Culture." *Change,* Jan./Feb. 1994, pp. 8–15.

Laidlaw, W. K. *Defining Scholarly Work in Management Education.* St. Louis: American Assembly of Collegiate Schools of Business, 1992.

Owens, R. G. *Organizational Behavior in Schools.* Englewood Cliffs, N.J.: Prentice Hall, 1970.

Pister, K. S. *Report of the Universitywide Task Force on Faculty Rewards.* Oakland: Office of the President, University of California, Berkeley, 1991.

Rhodes, F.H.T. *The New American University. David Dodds Henry Series.* Urbana: University of Illinois, 1990.

Rice, R. E. "The New American Scholar: Scholarship and the Purposes of the University." *Metropolitan Universities Journal,* 1991, *1* (4), 7–18.

Roberts, A. O., Wergin, J. F., and Adam, B. E. "Institutional Approaches to the Issues of Reward and Scholarship 1993." In R. M. Diamond and B. E. Adam (eds.), *Recognizing Faculty Work: Reward Systems for the Year 2000.* New Directions for Higher Education, no. 81. San Francisco: Jossey-Bass, 1993.

Stewart, D. W. *Secondary Research: Information Sources and Methods.* Applied Social Research Methods Series, vol. 4. Newbury Park, Calif.: Sage, 1984.

Suskie, L. A. *Questionnaire Survey Research: What Works.* Resources for Institutional Research no. 6. Tallahassee, Fla.: Association for Institutional Research, 1992.

Yin, R. K. *Case Study Research: Design and Methods.* Applied Social Research Methods Series, vol. 5. Newbury Park, Calif.: Sage, 1984.

Yuker, H. E. *Faculty Workload: Research, Theory, and Interpretation.* ASHE-ERIC Higher Education Report no. 10. Washington, D.C.: The George Washington University School of Education and Human Development, 1984.

PETER J. GRAY *is director of evaluation and research at the Center for Instructional Development, Syracuse University.*

ROBERT M. DIAMOND *is assistant vice chancellor for instructional development and professor of instructional design, development, and evaluation at Syracuse University.*

Using the professional portfolio as a structure, faculty and administrators can work together to assign and assess faculty work in ways that meet the needs of faculty members, their unit, the students, the institution, and society.

Assigning and Assessing Faculty Work

Peter J. Gray, Bronwyn E. Adam, Robert C. Froh, Barbara A. Yonai

By defining faculty work in the form of a mission statement, as described in Chapter Five, we set the stage for the actual assignment and assessment of responsibilities both for individual faculty members and for academic units as a whole. The purpose of this chapter is to help institutional researchers work with a campus leadership team to develop ways to assign and assess faculty work that are consistent with their efforts to redefine faculty work as embodied in those mission statements. The following discussion offers a brief analysis of the current practice of assigning and assessing faculty work; discusses the issues involved in developing a process that is consistent with a broadened definition of faculty work; and suggests the characteristics of a structure—that is, the professional portfolio—that can facilitate the assignment and assessment of faculty work. Along the way, observations are made regarding how institutional researchers can support the development of a process of assigning and assessing responsibilities that is both collaborative and equitable.

Current Process of Assigning and Assessing Faculty Work

Unit administrators have pressure from above to meet a variety of institutional responsibilities and pressure from faculty to allow them control over how they spend their time. Ideally, the process of assigning and assessing faculty work should provide an overall balance in the time faculty spend working with students, on professional citizenship, in scholarly activity, and on professional service, both for individual faculty and at the unit level. However, it often does not work out that way.

In many cases, faculty members see themselves as entrepreneurs who independently negotiate their responsibilities with the academic unit administrator. Therefore, to use the term *assigning* to suggest how responsibilities are distributed within an academic unit may be inappropriate. Perhaps a better way to conceptualize the process is to say that most faculty negotiate with their unit leader how they spend their time within broad parameters of institutional and departmental expectations. This process of negotiation gives some faculty considerable influence over the focus and amount of their efforts in relation to the various areas of faculty work (working with students, on professional citizenship, in scholarly activity, and on professional service).

Based on interviews with chairs and leading faculty at four selective liberal arts colleges and two universities, Massey (1990) describes the *academic ratchet,* a process whereby faculty negotiate on a continuous basis for greater proportions of discretionary time in relation to time spent working with undergraduates. The process of negotiation begins when faculty are first hired and focuses totally on individuals. Over time, these independent, competitive, and entrepreneurial negotiations can make it difficult for academic units to cover the range of functions, roles, and activities that make up their responsibilities, especially those that involve working with students.

In addition, the star system, which involves special treatment of some new faculty (often based on their research record or promise), disenfranchises others in the unit, who feel that their contributions are not appropriately appreciated or rewarded. They may feel that they must either remain second-class citizens or go elsewhere to attain a better negotiating position. Given today's tight academic job market, however, people may also feel as though they are trapped in a place where they are not valued. As a result, general faculty morale can suffer, as can collegiality and the overall effectiveness of the unit.

Similarly, when it comes time to assess faculty work, a variety of individually negotiated arrangements often must be considered. This situation works against a consistent and equitable evaluation process and reward system. To a great extent, this is the case because faculty correctly perceive that certain functions, roles, and activities are more highly valued because they are the ones rewarded by the institution and by their professional colleagues. All of this variety puts unit administrators in a very difficult spot. They must negotiate with faculty individually to ensure that the responsibilities of the unit are adequately covered and they must use many different criteria for evaluating performance and distributing rewards.

In Chapter Five, it was suggested that institutional researchers work with a campus leadership team to develop model processes for defining faculty work. They can play this same role in relating faculty work, as defined in mission statements, to the preferences of faculty so that work assignments are made in a fair and equitable way. In so doing, institutional researchers should keep in mind the nature of faculty as independent entrepreneurs and the complexity of incentives and rewards that motivate the choices faculty make regarding the work they perform.

Professional Portfolio

The purpose of developing new institutional and unit mission statements is to define faculty work more clearly and in a broader way. Then, the negotiation of faculty assignments and assessment can occur in a context that is explicit about the relative importance of all different types of faculty functions, roles, and activities. As suggested in Chapter Five, the range of legitimate faculty work within a particular academic unit can be defined most articulately through an open dialogue among the unit administrator and the faculty. With the guidance of the institutional and unit mission statements, such a collective discussion can help to ensure that faculty work is equitably assumed by all members of the unit. Similarly, assessment of the functions, roles, and activities necessary to carry out the unit's mission is best done through collective discussion.

A movement away from focusing on individual preferences and toward a sense of collective responsibility, action, performance, and assessment can be fostered when faculty share with their colleagues in a structured way their visions of their own work. The professional portfolio provides a vehicle for the collective discussion of faculty work in that it can be used to make public the common vision of faculty members' work.

Broadening the range of legitimate faculty work supports the development of a local culture in which faculty make choices and negotiate assignments that reflect not just their individual preferences, but the expectations of their institutions, departments, and disciplines, as well as the needs of students and society. In addition, explicitly defining the relative importance of various aspects of faculty work provides the basis for a fair and equitable process of assessing faculty work and distributing rewards. However, rhetoric is not enough to modify faculty attitudes. Changes in institutional and unit cultures will come about only when formal and informal systems for assigning, assessing, and rewarding faculty work correspond with statements by campus leaders regarding the value of the faculty functions, roles, and activities embodied in the redefinition of faculty work.

Considered collectively, faculty members' portfolios constitute the range of faculty work assigned to the unit. These portfolios serve as an important means of assessing how well the whole unit is accomplishing its mission, as well as the quality of the contributions of individual faculty members. Looking across portfolios provides information about how well faculty work has been defined within a given unit and how well the assigning process meets the needs of all constituencies—that is, how equitable it is. Therefore, issues of equity with respect to workload also become more evident when portfolios are used.

Instead of viewing the assigning process as a means of negotiating individual rewards and punishments and, therefore, viewing individuals as winners and losers, the more public portfolio can force the negotiation process to reach an equitable balance of individual and institutional needs and desires

through compromises made by all concerned for the good of the unit. Portfolio assessment also provides a means of tracking development over time of
both individuals and academic units.

This more public record of faculty work assignments, results, and rewards
can lead to a greater sense of community and more collegial relations among
faculty, if handled properly. It may well be that Shulman's (1993) observations
for making teaching more valued are applicable to the full range of faculty
work. That is, the full range is not valued because it is removed from the community of scholars: "if we wish to see greater recognition and reward attached
to [a full range of faculty work], we must move [it] from its current private status to community property" (Shulman, 1993, p. 6). However, making this
change in the local faculty culture will not be easy.

The first important benefit of portfolio use is that it makes professional
work a part of the conversation among scholars. In deciding what should go
into a portfolio and how it should be evaluated, institutions and their academic units must address the questions of what is appropriate and effective faculty work and what standards should be set for campus practice. In addition,
in the process of selecting and organizing their portfolio materials, faculty think
hard about their work, a practice that in itself is likely to lead to improvement
in performance (Edgerton, Hutchings, and Quinlan, 1991).

Because the use of portfolios is unfamiliar to people in many academic
disciplines, the following questions often arise: What is a portfolio? What are
the main components of a portfolio? How can the contents of a portfolio be
judged? The remainder of this chapter is an attempt to answer these questions.

What Is a Portfolio? A portfolio, according to Webster's, is a "selection of
representative works" intended to document the activity of a faculty member
over a particular period of time and for a particular purpose. In defining the
time period and purpose of the portfolio, evaluators establish its boundaries.

It is important to emphasize the ideas of selection and of representative
works. Even at the beginning of a faculty member's career, there are many possible works, in the form of descriptions of activities and products, that can be
included in a portfolio, which in its briefest form may be a curriculum vitae
and letter of application for a faculty position. Behind even this portfolio, however, is a much larger store of works from which selections must be made in
order to create an accurate and appropriate picture of the faculty member.

This idea of a store of materials from which a set of representative works
is selected is a major feature of the portfolio concept. As part of the Syracuse
University Future Professoriate Project (conceived and directed by Leo Lam-
bert, acting dean of the Syracuse University Graduate School), graduate students in the philosophy department coined the term *piles and files*. That is,
from the piles of materials one collects over time, files are selected for particular purposes and are then organized into a portfolio.

What are the Main Components of a Portfolio? The level of detail and
the scope of information included in a portfolio vary tremendously depending

on its purpose and audience. This information must be organized to best serve the purposes of a given portfolio, such as a formative or summative purpose, and include three components: the context, a self-reflective statement, and a selection of representative works. Each is described in detail here.

Component 1: The context statement. Whether a professional portfolio is intended to make the case for promotion, tenure, or other summative decisions or to direct faculty development in a formative way, the first component should be a statement that sets the context for the assignment and assessment of faculty work. The statement of the context has three elements.

The first element is a brief summary of the institutional or unit mission statements as they apply to a given faculty member. As discussed in Chapter Five, institutional and unit mission statements describe in a general way the relevant functions, roles, and activities of faculty work in areas such as working with students, professional citizenship, scholarly activity, and professional service. It also was suggested that mission statements indicate the relative importance of the general areas, as well as that of the various specific functions, roles, and activities.

The range of legitimate faculty work and the relative importance of specific kinds of faculty work as described in the mission statements should be related to the responsibilities of the faculty member whose portfolio is in question. Of course, relevance and relative importance vary considerably from institution to institution, from unit to unit, and from individual to individual.

Assigning faculty work involves negotiating between the unit responsibilities and faculty members' preferences. Faculty work is motivated to a considerable extent by intrinsic rewards. As Bok (1993, p. 167) indicates, "no system of payment can substitute for genuine interest and concern." Also, as Sir William Taylor (1991) suggests, the "ultimate assurance of quality is conscience." Identifying the things that are intrinsically rewarding to faculty members is the focus of the following discussion.

Institutional researchers can help their institution's leadership team understand the importance of closely matching institutional and academic unit missions with faculty members' desire to pursue excellence through following their own strengths and interests. This matching can be facilitated by making public the collective intrinsic rewards of the faculty in the institution and in units. A project on intrinsic rewards, led by Syracuse University, encourages discussion among groups of faculty focused on memorable events in teaching. Faculty report being inspired by these conversations because such interaction allows them to share their goals and the experiences they find most rewarding in their teaching lives. These conversations seem to offer relief from the current pressures that have fractured faculty groups and left individuals with few opportunities to talk with their colleagues about their teaching experiences.

Institutional researchers, who have in the past provided specific information at the request of chief academic administrators, must expand their view of the audiences they serve. Working with a campus leadership team, institutional researchers can develop methods of collecting data using the method of focused discussion that is embodied in the project just described, for explicating the intrinsic rewards faculty members get from teaching and other aspects of their work. These methods can facilitate open and informed negotiations regarding the assignment of faculty work.

In summary, the initial element of the context statement should relate the mission of the unit and a given faculty member's responsibilities based on a clear understanding of his or her strengths and interests and the needs of the unit. This may take the form of specific assignments, in the case of a summative portfolio, and areas of development or developmental goals in the case of a formative portfolio.

The second element of the context description provides an overview of the faculty member's responsibilities since the last review and briefly summarizes past accomplishments and prior reviews as they relate to the institutional or unit missions and current responsibilities or goals. By drawing on their experience of developing executive summaries of studies they have conducted, institutional researchers can help to provide model overviews that strike a balance between being too general and vague and too specific and detailed.

The third element of the context statement consists of operational definitions for each aspect of assigned faculty work or the goals intended to guide developmental activities. Exhibit 6.1 provides an example of an operational definition of professional service. In essence, this element is a description of the ground rules by which summative and formative decisions are to be made.

These ground rules should be negotiated at the beginning of the period covered by the portfolio. For example, this might be at the beginning of the year in anticipation of annual performance review and merit pay decisions, at the time someone is hired in anticipation of promotion and tenure decisions, or at the beginning of a three-year period when a specific faculty development plan is created.

In general, the assessment of faculty work is guided by operational definitions that have three parts. The first is a rationale for a faculty member's specific responsibilities or developmental goals. This rationale states in very specific terms the reasons for selecting the faculty functions, roles, and activities that are the focus of the portfolio.

The second part of an operational definition is a statement of acceptable evidence for documenting the performance of assigned faculty work or the accomplishment of developmental goals. At the most general level, evidence may be materials from oneself, actual products and descriptions of faculty work, and descriptive and evaluative materials from others (Schore, cited in Edgerton, Hutchings, and Quinlan, 1991, pp. 7–8). Documentation can be from the following people: the faculty members themselves, other faculty members, experts in the discipline both on campus and off campus, administrators, current students and alumni, off-campus clients, employers of graduates, and

Exhibit 6.1. Operational Definition of Professional Service

Rationale
Faculty members can provide a wide range of expertise to their communities that may
not otherwise be available. In doing so, faculty members build positive relationships
between town and gown. These interactions can also provide faculty members with
opportunities to apply some of their theories to practice, continue or expand their
research, and provide students with internships, class projects, or research sites. In
addition, many disciplines view such service as an important part of a faculty member's
role.

Documentation
Professional service can include consulting with community agencies in a wide variety
of projects or activities. Some examples of documentation are as follows:
- Letters inviting the faculty member to participate in the project
- Description of the project and the faculty member's role
- Minutes or records of meetings and plans
- Lists of participants
- Materials prepared by the faculty member
- On-site feedback of faculty member's role
- Description of follow-up of activities in terms of articles, grant applications, funding, or project extension
- Letters of support from board members or other participants in the project
- Evaluation reports

Criteria and Standards
The criteria and standards applied to the assessment of professional service may
include the following:
- Effectiveness of an activity
- The extent to which scholarly expertise was used
- Scope of the project
- Perceived value of project to the community
- Application of the work to one's teaching or scholarship (for example, development of new course materials or involvement of graduate students in research opportunities)
- Novelty and innovativeness of the project
- Impact of the project on the community
- Number of invitations to participate in subsequent service projects

parents and community leaders. Information may take the form of personal
logs and journals, guided observations and performance checklists of live or
videotaped performances, structured individual or group interviews, surveys
and questionnaires, tests and performance appraisals, writings (published or
not), qualitative or narrative assignments, and administrative records.

Criteria and standards for judging the quality of faculty work or the accomplishment of developmental goals are the third part of an operational definition.
Criteria are general statements about the qualities that work must exhibit in
order for faculty members to be considered for various rewards. Such qualities
include depth; scope; originality; significance; thoroughness; clarity of expression; actual or potential impact; internal or external reputation; contribution to

theory, practice, or understanding; and reputation and selectivity of the forum or setting of presentation or publication (based on the Report of the Association for Education in Journalism and Mass Communication on the Definition of Scholarship in Journalism; see Diamond and Adam, in press). What is most important is that these criteria are clearly stated and documentable so that they may guide the actual assessment of faculty work or development goals using the standards of success. Standards may be stated in terms of the amount, level, or extent of the qualities of faculty work that merit certain rewards, such as how many or how much; how high, how good, or how selective; or how broad a reputation or how wide a contribution.

The example of an operational definition in Exhibit 6.1, including a rationale, description of possible documentation, and suggested criteria and standards related to professional service, may help to clarify these elements.

To summarize, including operational definitions in the professional portfolio context statement is an excellent way to make them accessible for use by individual faculty members to guide their actions and for use by an academic unit to determine whether the expectations, understandings, and agreements they represent are fair and equitable.

The role of the unit administrator is to negotiate the responsibilities of individual faculty members in a way that meets unit needs, institutional expectations, and faculty preferences. Sometimes this negotiation involves developing formal performance contracts or agreements, which include an indication of the rewards that will result from their successful fulfillment. In other cases, this negotiation is part of a process of reaching informal understandings regarding expectations and the consequence of meeting or not meeting them. These understandings and agreements become the basis—that is, they set the context—for action on the part of faculty members, the assessment of work, and the distribution of rewards.

Ideally, the context statement should stimulate the development of an action plan that describes the activities to be carried out, the time period over which they will occur, and the resources needed to implement and evaluate the work assigned or the goals and objectives that have been set. Thus, the context statement should be created long before the portfolio is assembled.

Based on their involvement with strategic and other forms of planned change (such as strategic planning, total quality management, management by objectives, and continuous quality improvement), institutional researchers may have considerable experience in developing work statements, goals and objectives, and the components of operational definitions. This experience can help them to create model statements for use by faculty and unit administrators to set the context for summative and formative portfolios.

Component 2: Self-reflective statement. The self-reflective statement should present the faculty member's point of view of the accomplishment of the responsibilities or goals described in the context. That is, the faculty member should provide a statement concerning her or his philosophy, perspective, or position regarding the aspects of faculty work or developmental goals that are the focus of the portfolio. In essence, the self-reflective statement makes the case for the faculty member's accomplishment of the responsibilities or goals set in the context (component 1 of the portfolio), which is then supported by the selection of representative work (component 3 of the portfolio).

The self-reflective statement might elaborate on the brief summary of past accomplishments in the context section. It would be appropriate here to describe any extenuating circumstances that inhibited accomplishment and any areas in which expectations or standards were exceeded. The self-reflective statement also should discuss the relationship of current responsibilities or developmental goals to the faculty member's long-term professional development.

The self-reflective statement is the most difficult, but in the end can be the most worthwhile component of a portfolio. Many faculty members have never thought through their philosophy, perspective, or position regarding the broad range of faculty work. By doing so as part of the process of developing a self-reflective statement, they gain a much clearer understanding of their faculty role and their place in the unit and institution. In addition, if these self-reflective statements are shared among faculty members, then the unit as a whole gains an understanding of how its members see themselves in relation to the unit. This mutual understanding can form the foundation for a much more collegial and equitable sharing of responsibilities.

Component 3: Selection of representative works. The third element of a portfolio consists of the documentation that was identified as being acceptable when the faculty member's responsibilities or goals were set. The documentation included in a portfolio should be a selection of representative works. That is, it does not have to include every piece of available information. Instead, it should contain only the information that illustrates or supports the faculty member's position as described in the self-reflective statement. Selection of the most appropriate information should be guided by the operational definitions that have been developed as part of the context statement. Relevant documentation may be organized around a brief listing of the faculty member's performance or accomplishments in relation to the assigned faculty work or developmental goals. This listing might be similar to a curriculum vitae.

The selection of representative works may include original source materials such as videotapes of teaching, published articles, or student work, or it may be evaluative critiques, reviews, observations, or comments by someone regarding the quality of the faculty member's performance as exemplified by original source materials. If the information is evaluative, it should be consistent with the operational definition's criteria and standards created as part of the context statement.

Institutional researchers are well aware that documentation involves making tangible sometimes quite intangible functions, roles, and activities. They understand that no one piece of information can provide the definitive assessment of faculty performance. They also know that considerable creativity and flexibility are often required to identify documentation that both accurately reflects faculty member's responsibilities or developmental activities and that is accessible and credible to those making decisions. They can help faculty and unit administrators realize how important this is by offering to develop model information collection procedures that use a variety of techniques and that gather information from many different sources over a long enough period of time to be able to document with reasonable confidence the quality of faculty work and the impact of any developmental changes. In this way, institutional researchers can help to ensure that faculty and unit administrators have reliable and valid information on which to base decisions.

How Can the Contents of a Portfolio Be Judged? The final question to be answered concerns the process of judging the work of a faculty member as embodied in the portfolio. The actual assessment of faculty work involves two steps. The first step is to design and use methods to collect information from a variety of sources about specific faculty performance or developmental activities. The second step in the assessment of faculty work is the evaluation of the evidence collected using the criteria and standards set when operational definitions were formulated. In this regard, the context statement provides the ground rules for making judgments about a faculty member's portfolio. The self-reflective statement provides the faculty member's perspective on the accomplishment of responsibilities or developmental goals. The selection of representative works provides the evidence appropriate to making summative or formative judgments regarding the quality of an individual faculty member's performance.

However, there are two other concerns related to evaluating portfolios that also must be addressed, especially if comparative judgments are to be made. One is determining the quality of the portfolio as a whole. The second is ascertaining the relative quality, merit, or worth of one faculty member's portfolio in comparison with that of another faculty member.

Overall Quality. Determining the overall quality of a portfolio means judging a faculty member's performance in general across all assigned responsibilities or developmental goals. In addition, the overall quality of a portfolio involves such aspects as its conceptual sophistication, the technical ability demonstrated by its construction, the variety of work presented, the physical presentation of the portfolio itself, and the extent to which the portfolio communicates the potential of the faculty member for high-quality future work (based on Syracuse University's School of Art and Design Portfolio Evaluation Form, 1994).

Of course, it is possible to present a very attractive portfolio with little substance. But as has been demonstrated in such areas as the arts and architecture, where thousands of portfolios are reviewed each year, as reviewers gain experience they become more and more discriminating and become increasingly able to identify portfolios that are both well-presented and substantive. Being able to judge a portfolio's overall quality is the precursor to making comparative judgments among portfolios.

Comparative Judgments. Assessing the overall quality of an individual portfolio within the context of an agreed-on scope of work is difficult enough, but making comparative judgments of quality for purposes of awarding merit pay increases, reappointments, and other personnel decisions is especially complex. Therefore, in order to maintain faculty morale and to avoid possible serious legal implications, extreme care must be taken in establishing the procedures for making comparative decisions based on professional portfolios (or on any other basis, for that matter). In this regard, certain recommendations can be made for reviewing portfolios of faculty work:

Specify expected length for individual items or for the entire portfolio. Remember that it is a selection of representative works. Make sure that faculty feel comfortable with the specified length and understand the need to limit reading time for fairness to faculty across portfolios, as well as to reviewers.

Think carefully about criteria and standards and how readers will apply them to evidence in the portfolio. Establish qualities that can be demonstrated readily in the evidence faculty will provide.

Consider how comparative judgments will be made and reported back to faculty. The more gradations you decide on, the more difficult it is to make distinctions. Consider the features of each category you plan to include. What will differentiate a rating of 2 from 1 in your assessment? How will you explain those distinctions to faculty who have not had the benefit of comparative reading? Strong and weak portfolios are fairly easy to distinguish. It's in the middle that distinctions are very difficult.

Consider training or orientation time for portfolio reviewers. The cultivated type of reading described earlier with respect to the arts and architecture comes over time. Plan for practice, such as reading and norming sessions, that can help reviewers become more adept at reading for quality.

Publish and circulate all statements and criteria more than once. Provide sample documents (such as reflective statements) or complete portfolios for guidance as faculty prepare their portfolios.

If appropriate, consider establishing procedures for appeals.

Plan for ongoing review and revision of the assessment process.

Because they have experience with making sensitive judgments in many other areas, institutional researchers can help to create a model portfolio review process that is fair and equitable.

Meta-Review

The information gathered through the creation of a professional portfolio has obvious value for organizing evidence related to the evaluation of individual faculty work. Portfolios, however, also can provide valuable information about the accomplishment of the unit's mission and about the fair and equitable distribution and rewarding of work within a unit. Institutional researchers can help the campus leadership team develop a process of meta-review within and across units with the express purpose of evaluating the extent to which institutional and unit missions were accomplished and the faculty treated fairly and equitably. This type of meta-review is very different from the review of individual cases conducted by a campus promotion and tenure committee. The meta-review is intended to facilitate a collegial conversation about the whole range of legitimate faculty work and its support of the purposes and values of the campus community.

Conclusion

Institutional researchers can help to change the way faculty work is defined, assigned, and assessed by helping to develop model procedures, practices, and products that can be adopted by units across campus as they strive to change their local culture. The collegial culture of many campuses forms an ethos with which most faculty identify. Developing or reinforcing collegial strategies can move the faculty culture away from competition and toward a sense of collective responsibility.

References

Bok, D. C. *The Cost of Talent: How Executives and Professionals are Paid and How it Affects America.* New York: Free Press, 1993.

Diamond, R. M., and Adam, B. E. (eds.). *Statements from the Disciplines: The Work of Faculty.* Washington, D.C.: American Association for Higher Education, in press.

Edgerton, R., Hutchings, P., and Quinlan, K. *The Teaching Portfolio: Capturing the Scholarship in Teaching.* Washington, D.C.: American Association for Higher Education, 1991.

Massey, W. S. *A New Look at the Academic Department.* Philadelphia: Pew Higher Education Research Program, June 1990.

Shulman, L. S. "Teaching as Community Property." *Change,* Nov./Dec. 1993.

Syracuse University School of Art and Design. *Portfolio Evaluation Form.* Syracuse, N.Y.: Syracuse University College of Visual and Performing Arts, 1994.

Taylor, W. Presentation at the European Association for Institutional Research Forum. Edinburgh, Scotland, Aug. 1991.

Peter J. Gray *is director of evaluation and research at the Center for Instructional Development, Syracuse University.*

Bronwyn E. Adam *is assistant project director at the Center for Instructional Development, Syracuse University.*

Robert C. Froh *is associate director of evaluation and research at the Center for Instructional Development, Syracuse University.*

Barbara A. Yonai *is associate in evaluation and research at the Center for Instructional Development, Syracuse University.*

Providing useful information for deans and department chairs has major implications for the role and professional preparation of institutional researchers.

Implications for Institutional Research

Mary K. Kinnick

The higher education enterprise is experiencing enormous pressure for change. Chapter authors describe deans and department chairs as pivotal players within their organizations in positions to help facilitate or render more problematic the change process that is underway.

This volume takes the position that much of this change will focus on the definition, facilitation, and assessment of student learning and on faculty culture and the redefinition of faculty work. These themes are appearing with increasing frequency in higher education literature.

Within this context of change, what kinds of information are useful to deans and department chairs and what roles can institutional researchers play in providing this information? Creswell and England remind us of the lack of a research base about these information needs. Despite this deficiency, collectively the authors provide us with some glimpses as well as several full portraits of what such useful information might look like and describe the roles institutional researchers can play in increasing access to and the use of such information by deans and chairs. Six themes emerge that have implications for institutional researchers: local needs assessments, data integrity and interpretation, collaboration, skills and knowledge bases, training and development role, and academic collegiality.

Assessing Local Information Needs

Creswell and England suggest that information needs vary by dean and chair role and by the purpose for the information. Deans and chairs, depending on local circumstance and individual inclination, can assume one or more of the following role orientations: faculty-oriented, manager, leader, discipline-oriented, and externally oriented. The authors identify and describe four purposes for using the information: to respond, monitor, plan, and make decisions.

Reviewing these roles and information use purposes, as well as the external forces affecting higher education and previous work on dean and chair information needs, Creswell and England offer a comprehensive information taxonomy, suggesting categories of information needed, the types of information that might be included, and examples of information sources. Their taxonomy provides deans, chairs, and institutional researchers with a place to begin as they conduct their own information needs assessments.

Complementing this taxonomy are the chapters by McMillan and by Gentemann, Fletcher, and Potter. They help to flesh out in greater detail information needed about current and future students and about student learning outcomes. Although institutional research offices typically collect an extensive amount of information about students (such as demographics, retention and graduation rates, and satisfaction with the educational experience), much of it is summarized at the institution level only. These authors argue that for information to be useful (that is, to be used), it must be disaggregated to the program and department levels. McMillan reminds us that especially useful are trend and comparative information (for example, across units within the same institution and with similar units at other institutions) and projections, such as job market demand.

Creswell and England call for institutional researchers to be data architects and information sorters. A local assessment phase, however, must begin the process, where a thorough understanding is gained of dean and chair roles and the purposes for the information. This needs assessment phase must precede the design stage for these data architects.

Ensuring Data Integrity and Interpreting Information

Institutional researchers are called on by several authors to play a role in ensuring data integrity and in assisting with the appropriate interpretation of the data. A read through the chapters makes clear that the time-honored institutional research role of ensuring the integrity of data is valued here. For example, issues of data reliability and validity are substantial when dealing with the construction and assessment of faculty portfolios. As we move to the use of a wider variety of approaches and tools to assess student learning, again tough issues of data reliability and validity emerge. Institutional researchers are well-positioned to play a critical role in ensuring the integrity of these kinds of data.

Institutional researchers must do more, however, than help to design information systems. McMillan and Gentemann, Fletcher, and Potter speak with the same voice when they emphasize the importance of helping deans and chairs to interpret data. McMillan argues that more is needed than simply linking departments to data bases. Institutional researchers must help deans and chairs understand the meaning of the data.

Gentemann, Fletcher, and Potter urge that the role of institutional researchers not end with the release of student assessment data. Interpretation of the data is critical, particularly when the assessment of student learning is viewed as part of an ongoing curriculum reform process that requires curricular change decisions by deans and chairs and their faculties. Although institutional researchers play a critical part in both the analysis and the interpretation of the data, Gentemann, Fletcher, and Potter caution that faculty and academic leaders also must be centrally involved in this analysis and interpretation process. For serious review and change to occur, deans, chairs, and the faculty must become immersed in the data. Austin provides many examples of ways deans and chairs can play a direct part in assessing the culture and climate of their own academic units and important roles of institutional researchers in such assessment.

An implication here is that institutional researchers cannot operate effectively from afar, either as data architects, data sorters, data compilers, or senders of data. They must maintain closer interaction and communication with those whose information needs they support. Because institutional research resources are scarce, however, ways must be found to maximize the support these professionals can offer. This leads to the next theme.

Working Collaboratively

All of the authors describe institutional researchers of the future working as part of collaborative teams, with deans and chairs, faculty, and other campus leaders. In particular, Gray and Diamond and Gray, Adam, Froh, and Yonai call for institutional researchers to work as members of a campuswide leadership team in the effort to redefine faculty work. They also describe an opportunity for a leadership role by institutional researchers as they serve on campuswide teams charged with developing early prototypes or models of how to assign and assess faculty work. These models, developed for particular academic units on campus, can then be used to guide development of policies and procedures in other academic units at the institution.

Gentemann, Fletcher, and Potter call for our institutions to develop as learning communities. They encourage institutional researchers, working with deans, chairs, and faculty, to model the collaborative process. A student learning-focused agenda increases the need for partnerships among institutional researchers, academic leaders, and faculty.

Austin describes how institutional researchers can collaborate with deans and chairs in planning and implementing studies designed to assess faculty culture. Deans and chairs as well as institutional researchers have distinct roles to play in this process. Institutional researchers have the advantage of distance and objectivity with respect to issues in particular academic units. As outsiders who understand academia, they can often see things that those closer to the situation cannot.

McMillan describes a set of information on and about students that must come from a variety of sources: centrally stored computerized information,

information collected at the program and department levels, special surveys of students, and data bases maintained by external agencies (such as the state employment division). Institutional researchers must work closely with deans and chairs first to define the information that is needed and then to coordinate their roles in data collection, analysis, and interpretation.

Expanding Skill and Knowledge Bases

For institutional researchers to play a significant role in providing the kinds of useful information detailed in this volume, they must increase their skill and knowledge in the following six areas: qualitative research methods, educational tests and measurements, adult learning theory and research, faculty culture and its assessment, the organizational change process, and educational evaluation.

Gentemann, Fletcher, and Potter, Austin, and Gray and Diamond all call for institutional researchers to have skills in both qualitative and quantitative research methods. In addition to expertise with survey research and quantitative methods, expertise with interviewing, focus groups, observation, and content analysis is needed.

With the increasing focus on the assessment of student learning and faculty work, individuals familiar with the development of reliable, valid, and ethical assessment tools and procedures are sorely needed. If institutional researchers have the relevant knowledge and skill, they are more likely to play a central role in these activities. Many institutional researchers must retool in the area of student assessment. Their initial preparation in educational measurement, with its traditional emphasis on standardized tests and multiple-choice test forms, is no longer adequate. Institutional researchers must learn more about new and alternative assessment methods such as the construction and use of portfolios, performance-based measures, and self-assessment approaches.

According to Gentemann, Fletcher, and Potter, we need to move from a focus on disciplines and faculty teaching interests to a focus on student learning needs and how best to promote, facilitate, and assess that learning. All of us must understand more about adult learning and the assessment of that learning. Institutional researchers, as well as deans and chairs, must become more familiar with the adult learning literature.

Another literature that is likely to be unfamiliar to many institutional researchers is that on faculty culture and faculty work. Austin provides institutional researchers, deans, and department chairs with an introduction to the field. Gray and Diamond and Gray, Adams, Froh, and Yonai render the same service with respect to faculty work. Institutional researchers with experience primarily in faculty workload surveys and student credit hour and faculty contact hours analyses must retool.

When the focus is on organizational change, new tools and approaches are needed. Both Austin and Gray and Diamond see the change process focusing on faculty culture and faculty work. Gray and Diamond advocate and describe a planned change process. Several specific tools and approaches for use in assessing faculty culture and in redefining and assessing faculty work are described. Austin describes the academic workplace audit and the survey of faculty views. Gray, Adams, Froh, and Yonai describe a survey of campus culture and individual faculty perceptions developed at Syracuse University and provide a detailed description of the professional portfolio. Each of these tools and approaches can be adapted for use at different kinds of institutions and in different academic units.

Finally, Gray, Adams, Froh, and Yonai, writing about assigning and assessing faculty work, call on institutional researchers to conduct meta-analyses within and across units to evaluate the extent to which institutional and unit missions were accomplished and how fairly and equitably faculty were treated as a result of new processes. This evaluation adds a needed piece to the individual assessment of faculty work and contributes to an ongoing campuswide discussion about what constitutes legitimate faculty work.

Expanding Role in Training and Development

Over the past several years at Portland State University, I have watched institutional executives, confronted with shrinking resources, work creatively to streamline, downsize, and in some cases significantly decentralize former central administrative functions. In particular, we are currently decentralizing purchasing and other business office functions to departments using a new financial information system. New roles have emerged for business office staff. They are retooling and becoming adult educators. They are helping to train departmental secretaries, office staff, deans, and department chairs to use the new technology. They are serving in a support role as troubleshooters and also as auditors of the performance of the new system. A dramatic shift in roles has occurred for many of these staff members.

As I read through these chapters, a glimmer of a similar future role for institutional researchers emerged. Creswell and England, for example, call on institutional researchers to help deans and chairs understand the flow of information on their campuses, what is available, and how it can be accessed. McMillan calls on institutional researchers to help deans, chairs, and faculty understand more about the teaching and learning implications of various student characteristics.

Gentemann, Fletcher, and Potter specifically call for institutional researchers to help deans, chairs, and faculty to write student learning objectives and understand assessment alternatives and the technical characteristics of these tools. The image emerges of the future institutional researcher as an academic colleague who will play a role in providing professional development for deans and chairs, enabling them to better develop, access, and use information.

Establishing Academic Collegiality

The inclusion of this theme is not intended to suggest that current institutional researchers do not enjoy a collegial relationship with deans, chairs and faculty. Rather, inclusion of the theme is intended to underscore the importance of such a relationship.

As argued earlier, student learning, curriculum, and faculty work are viewed as the critical issues for academic leaders in U.S. colleges and universities. Although recent postsecondary education literature is filled with the language of accountability, quality and productivity, these issues fundamentally involve defining valued student learning, promoting and assessing this learning, and redefining and assessing faculty work.

To play a significant role in this arena requires a close and collegial relationship with deans, chairs, and faculty. In addition to their need for myriad technical computer-based and research skills, institutional researchers must demonstrate an understanding of the academic organization, the faculty culture, and the teaching and learning process. They must be viewed as trustworthy colleagues who can bring both their considerable technical talents and a sorely needed impartial perspective to highly charged settings and issues.

Conclusion

Collectively, the authors urge institutional researchers to learn more about the challenges facing deans and department chairs and to work as partners with them to provide information that can help them meet these challenges. To respond effectively, to develop truly useful information, institutional researchers must extend their current knowledge and skill base. In particular, they must understand more about student learning and its assessment and about faculty culture and faculty work. They must understand more about dean and department chair roles.

My hope is that this volume has at least in part fulfilled its major purpose: to increase the attention the institutional research community gives to the information needs of deans and department chairs. My further hope is that our institutions will be encouraged to make a greater effort to provide these frontline leaders with the information they need to meet the challenges facing their institutions.

MARY K. KINNICK is professor of education and chair, Department of Educational Policy, Foundations, and Administrative Studies in the School of Education, Portland State University, Portland, Oregon.

INDEX

ORDERING INFORMATION

NEW DIRECTIONS FOR INSTITUTIONAL RESEARCH is a series of paperback books that provides planners and administrators in all types of academic institutions with guidelines in such areas as resource coordination, information analysis, program evaluation, and institutional management. Books in the series are published quarterly in spring, summer, fall, and winter and are available for purchase by subscription as well as by single copy.

SUBSCRIPTIONS for 1994 cost $47.00 for individuals (a savings of 25 percent over single-copy prices) and $62.00 for institutions, agencies, and libraries. Please do not send institutional checks for personal subscriptions. Standing orders are accepted.

SINGLE COPIES cost $15.95 when payment accompanies order. (California, New Jersey, New York, and Washington, D.C., residents please include appropriate sales tax.) Billed orders will be charged postage and handling.

DISCOUNTS FOR QUANTITY ORDERS are available. Please write to the address below for information.

ALL ORDERS must include either the name of an individual or an official purchase order number. Please submit your order as follows:
    Subscriptions: specify series and year subscription is to begin
    Single copies: include individual title code (such as IR78)

MAIL ALL ORDERS TO:
    Jossey-Bass Publishers
    350 Sansome Street
    San Francisco, CA 94104-1342

FOR SUBSCRIPTION SALES OUTSIDE OF THE UNITED STATES, CONTACT: any international subscription agency or Jossey-Bass directly.